Kathryn Slocombe

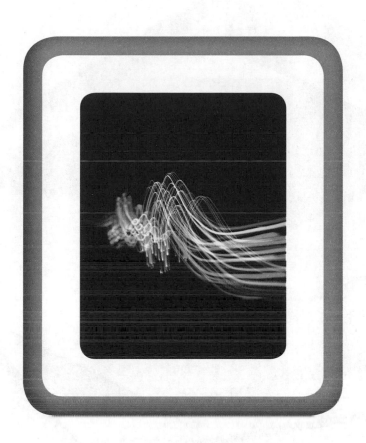

ESSENTIALS

GCSE AQA

Antholoav: Relationships

Acknowledgements

The author and publisher are grateful for permission to use quoted materials:

p.4–5, 46 'The Manhunt' by Simon Armitage, from *The Not Dead* (Pomona, 2008), reprinted by permission of Pomona Books.

p.6, 42–43, 46 'Hour' by Carol Ann Duffy, from *Rapture* (Picador, 2005). Copyright ©Carol Ann Duffy 2000, reprinted by permission of Pan Macmillan, London.

p.8–9, 46 'In Paris with You' by James Fenton, from *New Selected Poems* (Penguin, 2006), copyright ©James Fenton 2006. Reprinted by permission of United Agents on behalf of: James Fenton.

p. 10–11, 46 'Quickdraw' by Carol Ann Duffy, from *Rapture* (Picador, 2005). Copyright ©Carol Ann Duffy 2000, reprinted by permission of Pan Macmillan, London.

p.12, 36–37, 39 'Ghazal' by Mimi Khalvati, Carcanet Press Limited, copyright Mimi Khalvati 2006.

p.14, 40–41, 46 'Brothers' by Andrew Forster, from *Fear of Thunder* (Flambard Press, 2007), reprinted by permission of the publisher.

p.16, 46 'Praise Song for My Mother' by Grace Nichols, from *The Fat Black Woman's Poems* (Virago, 1984). Reproduced with permission of Curtis Brown Group Ltd, London on behalf of Grace Nichols. Copyright © Grace Nichols, 1984.

p.18, 46 'Harmonium' by Simon Armitage, ©Simon Armitage 2009, reproduced by permission of David Godwin Associates Ltd.

p.30, 47 'Nettles' by Vernon Scannell, from *The Very Best of Vernon Scannell* (Macmillan, 2001), reprinted with kind permission of the Literary Executor for the Estate of Vernon Scannell.

p.32, 42–43 'Born Yesterday' by Philip Larkin, from *The Less Deceived* (Faber, 2011), © Philip Larkin, reprinted by permission of the publishers, Faber & Faber Ltd.

Contents

The Manhunt

About the Poem

- Written by **Simon Armitage** (1963–).

- The poem describes a woman's attempts to rebuild her relationship with her husband, an injured soldier who has returned home from war.

- The poem explores the effects of the husband's injuries on his relationship with his wife.

- The distance between the couple is evident from the title, as the wife searches for her husband who has been lost to her.

Ideas, Themes and Issues

- **Trust:** Even though the damage to the relationship was not caused by the husband or wife, the wife needs to regain her husband's trust before he will allow her to see his vulnerability.

- **Pain:** There's a clear sense of physical and emotional pain.

- **Love and marriage:** The wife's gentle persistence to reclaim her husband and heal their relationship reveals the strength of her commitment to him.

The Manhunt

This brings to mind the initial passionate reunion but implies this is a passing phase.

> After the first phase,
> after passionate nights and intimate days,

These repeated words suggest the wife's tireless efforts to regain her husband's trust.

> only then would he let me trace
> the frozen river which ran through his face,
>
> 5 only then would he let me explore
> the blown hinge of his lower jaw,

The repetitive structure of two verbs joined by 'and' reminds us of the wife's persistence in attempting to reconnect with her husband.

> and handle and hold
> the damaged, porcelain collar-bone,
>
> and mind and attend
> 10 the fractured rudder of shoulder-blade,

The clustering together of the repeated words in one stanza emphasises the wife's determination.

> and finger and thumb
> the parachute silk of his punctured lung.
>
> Only then could I bind the struts
> and climb the rungs of his broken ribs,

Key Features

Repetition	Full rhyme	Verbs

Verbs • Emphatic • Metaphor • Juxtaposition

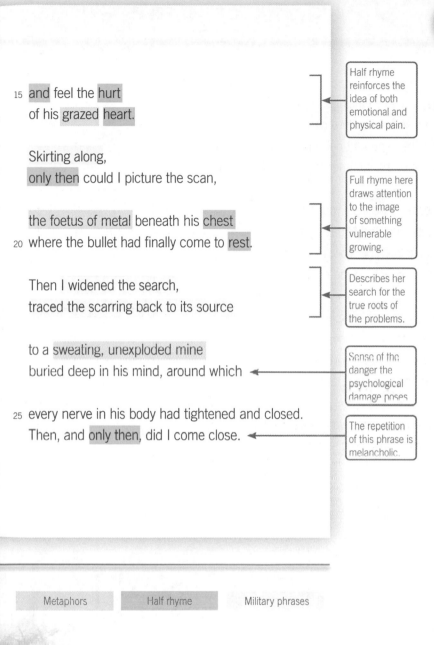

15 and feel the hurt
of his grazed heart.

Skirting along,
only then could I picture the scan,

the foetus of metal beneath his chest
20 where the bullet had finally come to rest.

Then I widened the search,
traced the scarring back to its source

to a sweating, unexploded mine
buried deep in his mind, around which

25 every nerve in his body had tightened and closed.
Then, and only then, did I come close.

> Half rhyme reinforces the idea of both emotional and physical pain.

> Full rhyme here draws attention to the image of something vulnerable growing.

> Describes her search for the true roots of the problems.

> Sense of the danger the psychological damage poses.

> The repetition of this phrase is melancholic.

Metaphors   Half rhyme   Military phrases

Form, Structure and Language

- **Irregular rhyme** reflects the fluctuations in the closeness between the couple.

- **Repetition** is used to show the husband's hesitation and his wife's persistence in healing the relationship.

- The **verbs** become more **emphatic** as he allows her closer, but also suggest the wife's tenderness.

- A series of **metaphors** describe the husband's injured body, emphasising his physical frailty.

- Tension is created through the **juxtaposition** of sensuous, tactile descriptions and references to pain and injury.

- The shorter lines of the eighth **stanza** highlight the wife's **empathy**. They draw attention to an image with both physical and romantic **connotations**.

- The wife's use of military-sounding phrases links her to her husband and echoes the title.

- The psychological impact of his experiences is clear. The final line is melancholic as the wife acknowledges the distance that remains between them.

Quick Test

1 Which materials are used to describe the husband's body and what do they suggest about it?

2 How does the poet create a sense of the wife's persistence?

3 How is the tenderness the wife shows suggested?

Hour

Read aloud, this is a homophone ('hour'/'our') suggesting the poem's concerns with time and intimacy.

Hour

Love's time's beggar, but even a single hour,
bright as a dropped coin, makes love rich.
We find an hour together, spend it not on flowers
or wine, but the whole of the summer sky and a grass ditch.

5 For thousands of seconds we kiss; your hair
like treasure on the ground; the Midas light
turning your limbs to gold. Time slows, for here
we are millionaires, backhanding the night

so nothing dark will end our shining hour,
10 no jewel hold a candle to the cuckoo spit
hung from the blade of grass at your ear,
no chandelier or spotlight see you better lit

than here. Now. Time hates love, wants love poor,
but love spins gold, gold, gold from straw.

Emphasises how they value each moment.

Midas's wish left him alone, hungry and begging to be freed. This reference suggests the couple's eventual separation.

Images of darkness suggest lurking problems.

Out of place image creates bathos. It is unique and personal. See also 'grass ditch'.

The enjambment and caesura focus our attention on the here and now, just as the couple are focused on them.

A reference to Rumpelstiltskin, suggesting greed and betrayal.

Key Features

Wealth	Near rhyme	Light	First person plural	Time	Myth / folk tale

Homophone • Sonnet • Metre • First person

About the Poem

- Written by **Carol Ann Duffy** (1955–).

- The poem describes a snatched moment of time that two lovers spend together.

- The couple luxuriate in their time together and find the most mundane things beautiful and romantic.

- The poem is part of a collection of poems called *Rapture*, charting the life of a romantic relationship. *Hour* describes the early stages of the relationship. *Quickdraw* is also part of this collection.

Ideas, Themes and Issues

- **Love**: Presented as an enriching, **enlightening** experience. However, there are subtle hints that even in this relationship, tensions and problems lurk just below the surface.

- **Time**: Traditionally, time is seen as the enemy of lovers, but in this poem the power of their love means that it has little impact on them.

- **Sex**: The physical pleasure and passion that often characterises the early stages of a relationship is clear through references to kissing and the focus on the lover's body.

Form, Structure and Language

- The title reveals one of the poem's main concerns and acts as a **homophone** for the couple's experience.

- The poem is written in **sonnet** form, but alterations to the usual **metre** and **rhyme** may suggest underlying tensions in the relationship.

- The use of the **first person plural** reflects that the experience is shared and suggests the unity of the couple.

- The **extended metaphor** linking their relationship to riches and treasure shows they are enriched by their time together.

- The rejection of traditional symbols of romance in favour of more mundane things creates **bathos**. The unique things they notice reflect the intimate nature of their relationship.

- References to myths and folk tales create the impression of a fairy tale romance, but the themes of the stories could be seen to **foreshadow** the end of the relationship.

- The emphasis on the single word 'Now' in the final **stanza** reinforces that the couple are living in the present moment.

Quick Test

1. How does the poet suggest that the lovers are enriched by this relationship?

2. Which images seem at odds with the more expected symbols of romance?

3. Which myths and folk tales are mentioned in the poem and what does this suggest about the relationship?

4. What is the effect of the half-rhyme of the final couplet?

Extended metaphor • Bathos • Foreshadow • Stanza

In Paris with You

About the Poem

- Written by **James Fenton** (1949–).

- The voice in the poem has just experienced the end of a relationship and is in Paris with a new partner.

- There's no desire to see the romantic sights of Paris; instead he wants to enjoy the moment for what it is.

- By the end of the poem, it seems that the voice has stronger feelings for the person he is with, although he is reluctant to admit it to them.

Ideas, Themes and Issues

- **Romance**: The poem is set in one of the most romantic cities in the world. The romantic sights are named and rejected, which suggests he is rejecting the emotional attachment of a serious relationship.

- **Self-discovery**: The voice in the poem seems to have lost sight of himself in his previous relationship. Often, people sacrifice parts of themselves to make a relationship work. There's an element of self-discovery in the new relationship.

- **Sex**: The voice in the poem has no interest in the sights of Paris and prefers to stay in the hotel room. There is a veiled, but clear, reference to sex in the final **stanza**.

The negativity he feels is apparent from the outset.

These light-hearted images combine to suggest he has been held back by the previous relationship.

The lack of conjunction suggests he is becoming more focused on the present relationship.

The shorter lines stand out, focusing attention on their exploration of each other.

In Paris with You

Don't talk to me of love. I've had an earful
And I get tearful when I've downed a drink or two.
I'm one of your talking wounded.
I'm a hostage. I'm maroonded.
5   But I'm in Paris with you.

Yes I'm angry at the way I've been bamboozled
And resentful at the mess I've been through.
I admit I'm on the rebound
And I don't care where are *we* bound.
10 I'm in Paris with you.

Do you mind if we do *not* go to the Louvre,
If we say sod off to sodding Notre Dame,
If we skip the Champs Elysées
And remain here in this sleazy
15   Old hotel room
Doing this and that
To what and whom
Learning who you are,
Learning what I am.

Key Features

Internal rhyme   Colloquial language   Play on words

20 Don't talk to me of love. Let's talk of Paris,
    The little bit of Paris in our view.
    There's that crack across the ceiling
    And the hotel walls are peeling
    And I'm in Paris with you.

25 Don't talk to me of love. Let's talk of Paris.
    I'm in Paris with the slightest thing you do.
    I'm in Paris with your eyes, your mouth,
    I'm in Paris with… all points south.
    Am I embarrassing you?
30 I'm in Paris with you.

This line reflects his changing emotions. The metonymy is clear – to protect himself he replaces 'love' with 'Paris'.

These images suggest he is distracting himself from his developing feelings.

Anaphora suggests the developing emotion he is feeling.

Conjunctions   Negative language   Metonymy

Form, Structure and Language

- **Colloquial** language suggests we are listening in to someone's thoughts or one side of a conversation.

- The **play on words** and unusual language creates a comic tone, which contrasts with the initial tone.

- The made-up word 'maroonded' has been manipulated to fit the rhyme scheme, which could reflect how he felt he was treated in his last relationship.

- The unexpected **internal rhyme** highlights the emotions of the speaker.

- **Conjunctions** show the changing nature of his feelings.

- Unusual **syntax** sounds almost questioning, suggesting uncertainty about the nature of the relationship.

- The opening line is echoed in the fourth and fifth stanzas, but is softened by the **metonymy**.

- The ending is **ambiguous**. We are not sure whether the comment reflects the location, or is an example of metonymy.

Quick Test

1. Why does the voice in the poem 'talk of Paris', rather than love?
2. What does the phrase 'sleazy / Old hotel room' imply about the trip to Paris?
3. What is the effect of the colloquial language in the poem?
4. What is the significance of the final line?

Syntax • Metonymy

Key Words 9

Quickdraw

The conceit is apparent from the title and implies a showdown between the couple. Images linked to Westerns recur throughout the poem.

Caesura in these lines highlights danger and isolation.

An element of showmanship suggests this is almost a game. Her comments do not hurt her opponent.

The impact of the lover's words is clear.

The metaphor shows the kiss is the source of the pain, but we are not sure of the intention behind it.

Quickdraw

I wear the two, the mobile and the landline phones,
like guns, slung from the pockets on my hips. I'm all
alone. You ring, quickdraw, your voice a pellet
in my ear, and hear me groan.

₅
                          You've wounded me.
Next time, you speak after the tone. I twirl the phone,
then squeeze the trigger of my tongue, wide of the mark.
You choose your spot, then blast me

                        through the heart.

₁₀ And this is love, high noon, calamity, hard liquor
in the old Last Chance saloon. I show the mobile
to the Sheriff; in my boot, another one's

concealed. You text them both at once. I reel.
Down on my knees, I fumble for the phone,
₁₅ read the silver bullets of your kiss. Take this …
and this … and this … and this … and this …

Her reaction to the call is swift, instinctive.

The length and placement of the lines add to their impact. The image of the heart has romantic connotations.

List of images suggest the point of no return.

The effect of the words is clear – the voice in the poem is seriously affected by the lover's words.

Key Features

Present tense   Initial caesura   Western images   Ambiguity   Internal rhyme   Terminal caesura

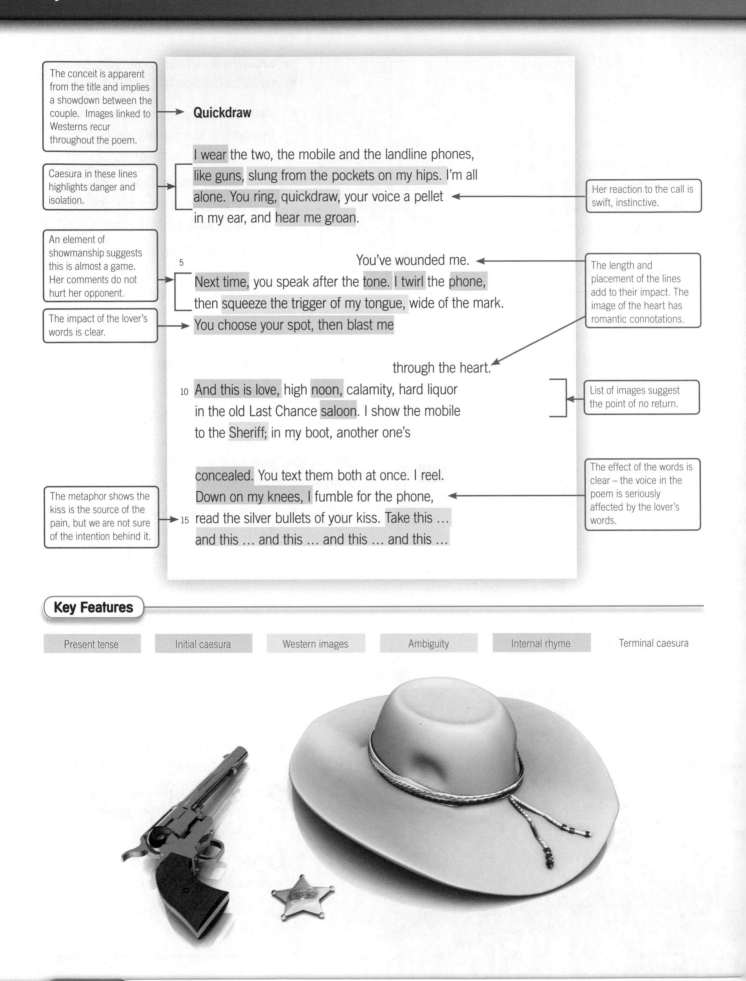

About the Poem

- Written by **Carol Ann Duffy** (1955–).

- An argument between lovers is portrayed using the **conceit**, or **extended metaphor**, of a Western gunfight. The lovers are fighters with phones and voices as their weapons.

- The lovers fire words at each other, with the intention of causing pain.

- The end of the poem is ambiguous; we're not sure if the kisses are violent or loving.

- This poem and *Hour* are part of a collection of poems charting a romantic relationship. *Quickdraw* marks the half-way point in the collection and the relationship.

Ideas, Themes and Issues

- **Passion and pain**: The two ideas are closely linked in the poem and the ambiguity in some of the lines makes it difficult to tell which is being described. Often, as a relationship nears its end, there is a point where desire remains even though the people in the relationship hurt each other.

- **Power**: While they are both trying to hurt the other person, it seems the power in this relationship is one-sided. The speaker seems less sure of herself than her 'target' and suffers more wounds than the 'opponent'.

Form, Structure and Language

- The poem is written in **free verse** with the mix of **enjambment** and **caesura** creating an uneven rhythm. This reflects the erratic nature of arguments.

- The argument is given immediacy through the use of the present tense.

- In the first **stanza**, the **initial caesura** highlights the conceit and emphasises the speaker's isolation.

- Tension is created through varied sentence lengths and **internal rhyme** in the second stanza.

- The **alliteration** of **plosive** sounds mimics the hardness of the bullets.

- **Ambiguity** leaves us unsure whether her reaction to the voice on the phone is pleasure, pain or both. This suggests that relationships sometimes create a mixture of positive and negative feelings for the people in them.

- The **terminal caesura** in the final stanza adds to the impact of the short phrase. The effect is sharp and unexpected.

Quick Test

1. What do the lovers use as weapons in this fight?

2. Which image suggests that there is little hope for the relationship?

3. What is interesting about the way lines 5 and 9 are presented? Why do you think Duffy did this?

4. What is the effect of caesura and enjambment in the poem?

Alliteration • Plosive • Terminal caesura

Ghazal

This sher's images of nature suggest the relationship is natural, reciprocal and sexual.

In each sher, the rhyming word describes the lover's action and the refrain (repeated word) is 'me'.

Reference to Eros's arrow suggests it is only a matter of time before they give in.

The images suggest both a threat and a challenge.

In the myth Daphne transformed into a laurel tree in order to protect herself from the attentions of men. Apollo embraced the tree then took the laurel as his emblem to show his love for her.

Suggests eternal youth, rest and eroticism.

Ghazal

If I am the grass and you the breeze, blow through me.
If I am the rose and you the bird, then woo me.

If you are the rhyme and I the refrain, don't hang
on my lips, come and I'll come too when you cue me.

5 If yours is the iron fist in the velvet glove
when the arrow flies, the heart is pierced, tattoo me.

If mine is the venomous tongue, the serpent's tail,
charmer, use your charm, weave a spell and subdue me.

If I am the laurel leaf in your crown, you are
10 the arms around my bark, arms that never knew me.

Oh would that I were bark! So old and still in leaf.
And you, dropping in my shade, dew to bedew me!

What shape should I take to marry your own, have you
– hawk to my shadow, moth to my flame – pursue me?

15 If I rise in the east as you die in the west,
die for my sake, my love, every night renew me.

If, when it ends, we are just good friends, be my Friend,
muse, lover and guide, Shamsuddin to my Rumi.

Be heaven and earth to me and I'll be twice the me
20 I am, if only half the world you are to me.

A play on words suggesting both her willingness to change herself and a reference to marriage.

She likens herself to the moon, a symbol of the female. He is the sun – linking to the next sher as 'Shamsuddin', translates as 'sun of the faith'.

After meeting Shamsuddin, Rumi spent 10 years writing ghazals.

The end of the relationship is expected – realistic but unusual for love poetry.

The final sher emphasises how important the lover is to the voice in the poem.

Key Features

| Conditional | Long vowels | Refrain | Full rhyme | References to poetry | Pun |

Metaphor • Conditional

About the Poem

- Written by **Mimi Khalvati** (1944–).
- The ghazal is a form of poetry that is structured in two-line **shers**, or verses. In the first sher, the first and second lines share the same final word. This word then ends each subsequent sher.

- Each sher can stand alone, but also contributes to the overall meaning of the ghazal.
- A single rhyme and metre runs throughout the entire poem.
- 'Ghazal' means 'lover's exchanges' in Arabic.

Ideas, Themes and Issues

- **Passion, desire and sex**: The poem is full of **metaphors** which suggest desire, and many have erotic undertones. The desire in this poem seems one-sided and it's not clear if the feelings are reciprocated or if the person it is addressed to even knows how the voice in the poem feels.

- **Poetry**: There are many references to poetry: the voice in the poem links both herself and the object of her affections to the form of the poem; the laurel leaf is said to be an embodiment of the spirit of prophecy and poetry; she links herself to Rumi, a 13th century Persian poet.

Form, Structure and Language

- The repeated use of the **conditional** creates a wistful tone.
- In the first **sher**, the long vowel sounds mimic what they describe.
- In the second sher the form and content are interwoven. This may reflect how the voice of the poem sees herself and the object of her affection.
- The language used to describe the lover's actions is active and seductive.
- The image of the laurel leaf could be interpreted as a **symbol** of eternal love or as an embodiment of the spirit of prophecy and poetry.

- The seventh sher suggests an almost irresistible but dangerous attraction.
- The penultimate sher stands out as both the rhyme and **refrain** are altered, emphasising the importance of the image. The relationship is a turning point in their lives.
- The final sher contains the poet's signature in a **pun**. It also suggests that the feelings in the relationship are not equal.

Quick Test

1. Explain the line 'If you are the rhyme and I the refrain'.
2. What does the phrase, 'arms that never knew me' suggest?
3. What do the images of Shamsuddin and Rumi suggest about the lovers?
4. The rhyming words describe what the voice of the poem wants the lover to do. What connects these words and what do they suggest about her desires?

Brothers

Brothers

The opening leaves us in no doubt that the voice in the poem sees his brother's company as a burden.

Saddled with you for the afternoon, me and Paul
ambled across the threadbare field to the bus stop,
talking over Sheffield Wednesday's chances in the Cup
while you skipped beside us in your ridiculous tank-top,
5 spouting six-year-old views on Rotherham United.

Metaphor describing worn field. The detail suggests the clarity of the memory of the day.

This combined with 'spouting' shows the disdain he felt for his brother.

The adverb adds impact, emphasising the exaggerated, energetic movements of the younger brother.

Suddenly you froze, said you hadn't any bus fare.
I sighed, said you should go and ask Mum
and while you windmilled home I looked at Paul.
His smile, like mine, said I was nine and he was ten
10 and we must stroll the town, doing what grown-ups do.

The older boys act together. These lines also highlight their youth.

Ambiguous statements that could refer to his actions at the time – representing his opportunity to change the situation, or him looking back from an adult's perspective.

As a bus crested the hill we chased Olympic Gold.
Looking back I saw you spring towards the gate,
your hand holding out what must have been a coin.
I ran on, unable to close the distance I'd set in motion.

The ambiguity in this stanza could reflect the unresolved feelings of the voice in the poem as he looks back on this incident.

Key Features

| Grammar | Verbs (lethargy) | Verbs (energy) | Internal rhyme | Ambiguity | Caesura |

About the Poem

- Written by **Andrew Forster** (1964–).
- Describes the relationship between brothers.
- The voice in the poem recalls an incident from his childhood when he was stuck spending time with his younger brother.
- He and another older boy resented spending time with the younger child and took the first opportunity to escape from his company.
- Looking back at the incident from an adult's perspective, it seems to have great significance to the brothers' relationship.

Ideas, Themes and Issues

- **Siblings**: The older brother feels that the presence of his younger brother is a burden. Age gaps and differences in personalities can make sibling relationships difficult.
- **Childhood**: Children are often in a hurry to grow up and want to be thought of as adults. Young children live in the moment and give little thought to the consequences of their behaviour.
- **Regret**: The recollection of this incident and the tone of the poem suggest the older brother regrets his actions and regrets not having a closer relationship with his brother.

Form, Structure and Language

- Details of specific places and events signal that this poem recalls a particular, personal incident that played a part in shaping the relationship.
- A lack of **imagery** and the use of grammatically incorrect phrases create a realistic, conversational tone.
- The tone of the relationship is clear from the opening phrase and reveals that the older brother feels burdened by his younger sibling.
- **Verbs** that emphasise movement and energy suggest the younger brother's excitement at being with his older brother. This contrasts with the slow movements of the older boys.
- **Internal rhyme** sounds childish and highlights that despite feeling grown-up the older boys are still children themselves.
- The final **stanza** is the shortest. It concludes the narrative and reveals the lasting distance between the brothers.
- **Ambiguity** in the final stanza allows for different interpretations of the events; the adult's perspective and the child's.
- The **caesura** in the final line highlights the distance between the brothers.

Quick Test

1. Why is the opening line of the poem so important?
2. Find two verbs to describe the actions of the younger brother and two to describe the older brother.
3. How does the poet show that despite feeling grown-up the older brother is still young himself and why might these details have been included?

Praise Song for My Mother

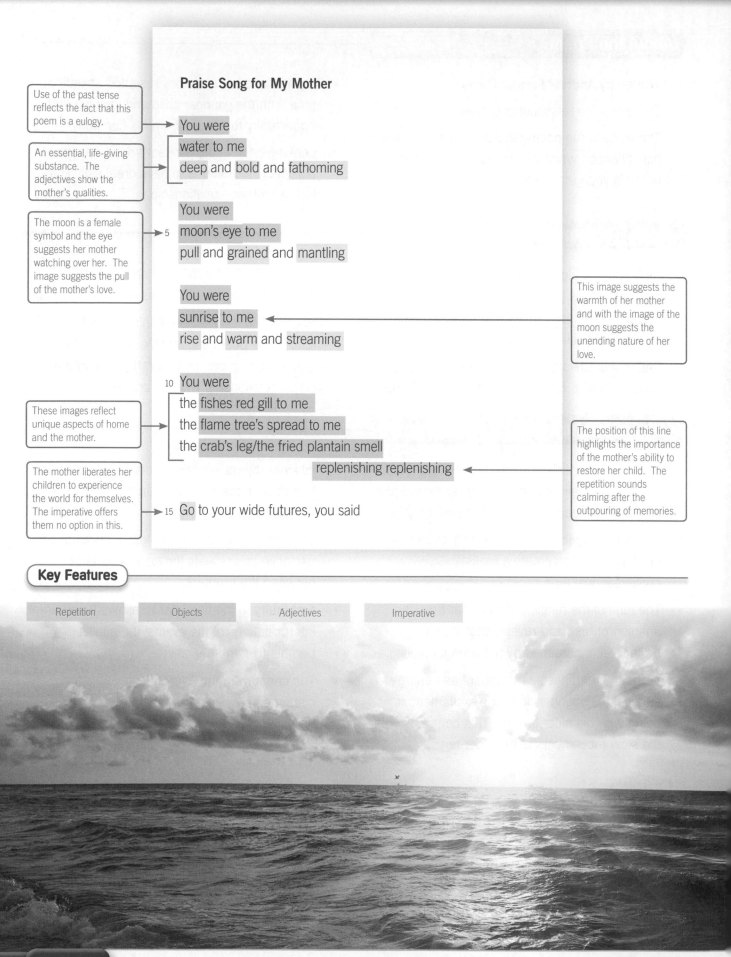

Praise Song for My Mother

Use of the past tense reflects the fact that this poem is a eulogy.

You were
water to me
deep and bold and fathoming

An essential, life-giving substance. The adjectives show the mother's qualities.

You were
5 moon's eye to me
pull and grained and mantling

The moon is a female symbol and the eye suggests her mother watching over her. The image suggests the pull of the mother's love.

You were
sunrise to me
rise and warm and streaming

This image suggests the warmth of her mother and with the image of the moon suggests the unending nature of her love.

10 You were
the fishes red gill to me
the flame tree's spread to me
the crab's leg/the fried plantain smell

These images reflect unique aspects of home and the mother.

replenishing replenishing

The position of this line highlights the importance of the mother's ability to restore her child. The repetition sounds calming after the outpouring of memories.

The mother liberates her children to experience the world for themselves. The imperative offers them no option in this.

15 Go to your wide futures, you said

Key Features

Repetition   Objects   Adjectives   Imperative

Praise Song for My Mother

About the Poem

- Written by **Grace Nichols** (1950–).
- A praise song is a traditional African form of poetry which **eulogises** the life of someone by comparing them to a range of different things.

- Nichols wrote this poem following the death of her mother. In the poem she explores what her mother means to her.

Ideas, Themes and Issues

- **Motherhood**: Motherhood is portrayed as essential, protecting, nourishing and liberating. It exerts a gentle, but permanent, pull between mother and child. The effects of this love continue to be felt even after the mother's death.

- **Love**: The mother's love is demonstrated by the things she does. Perhaps the most important way she reveals this love is by freeing her child for her future.

Form, Structure and Language

- The **repetition** of the opening line keeps the poem moving on despite the mother being recalled from memory.

- The first three **stanzas** are uniform in structure. The change in structure in the fourth stanza feels like an outpouring of memories and emotion.

- The **metaphor** in each stanza links the mother to something that symbolises Guyana, or to things particular to the mother.

- Three words follow each metaphor, the last of which is a **verb** used as an **adjective**. These words develop the image and explain the mother's qualities.

- **Repetition** of 'replenishing' slows the pace after the outpouring and shows how the mother's influence still restores her.

- The final line of the poem stands out and signifies the mother's lasting gift to her child.

- The poem contains no **punctuation**, which reflects the limitless love between mother and child and that the effects of that love are still felt.

Quick Test

1. What is the effect of the change in structure of the fourth stanza?
2. What is the role of the metaphors in the poem?
3. Why is there no punctuation in the poem?
4. What is the effect of the imperative in the final line of the poem?

Metaphor

Harmonium

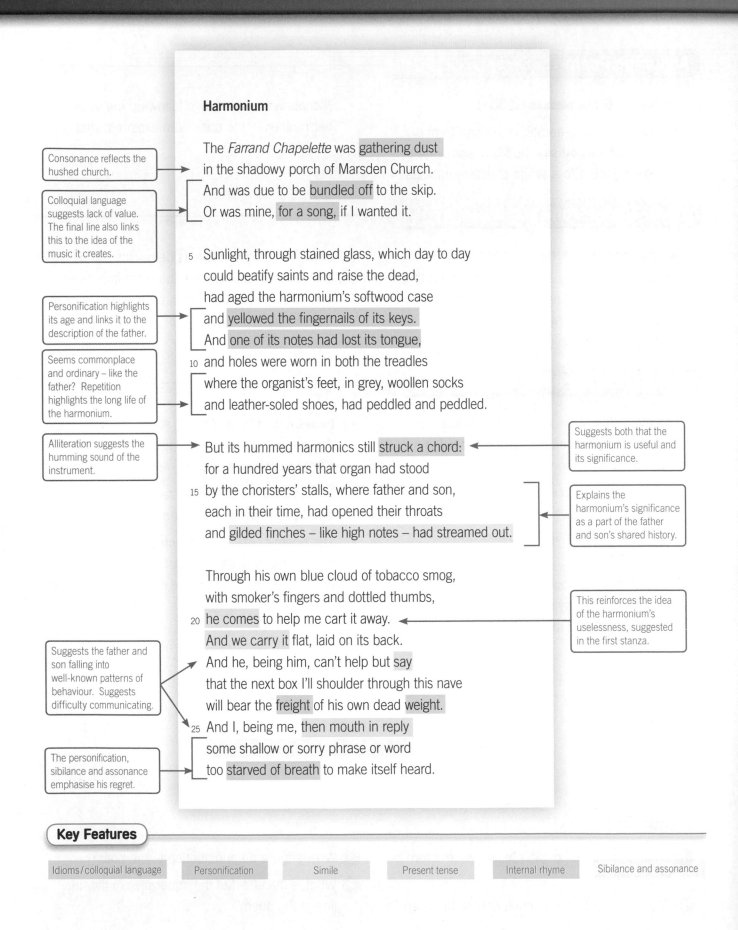

Harmonium

Consonance reflects the hushed church.

Colloquial language suggests lack of value. The final line also links this to the idea of the music it creates.

The *Farrand Chapelette* was gathering dust
in the shadowy porch of Marsden Church.
And was due to be bundled off to the skip.
Or was mine, for a song, if I wanted it.

5   Sunlight, through stained glass, which day to day
could beatify saints and raise the dead,
had aged the harmonium's softwood case

Personification highlights its age and links it to the description of the father.

and yellowed the fingernails of its keys.
And one of its notes had lost its tongue,
10 and holes were worn in both the treadles

Seems commonplace and ordinary – like the father? Repetition highlights the long life of the harmonium.

where the organist's feet, in grey, woollen socks
and leather-soled shoes, had peddled and peddled.

Alliteration suggests the humming sound of the instrument.

But its hummed harmonics still struck a chord:
for a hundred years that organ had stood
15 by the choristers' stalls, where father and son,
each in their time, had opened their throats
and gilded finches – like high notes – had streamed out.

Suggests both that the harmonium is useful and its significance.

Explains the harmonium's significance as a part of the father and son's shared history.

Through his own blue cloud of tobacco smog,
with smoker's fingers and dottled thumbs,
20 he comes to help me cart it away.
And we carry it flat, laid on its back.

This reinforces the idea of the harmonium's uselessness, suggested in the first stanza.

Suggests the father and son falling into well-known patterns of behaviour. Suggests difficulty communicating.

And he, being him, can't help but say
that the next box I'll shoulder through this nave
will bear the freight of his own dead weight.
25 And I, being me, then mouth in reply

The personification, sibilance and assonance emphasise his regret.

some shallow or sorry phrase or word
too starved of breath to make itself heard.

Key Features

Idioms/colloquial language   Personification   Simile   Present tense   Internal rhyme   Sibilance and assonance

About the Poem

- Written by **Simon Armitage** (1963–).
- This poem explores the relationship between a father and son.
- It describes a specific location and event, so feels personal.

- The title refers to an old, disused harmonium that the son sees and rescues from a church.
- The harmonium is a symbol of their relationship. It brings up memories of their shared history and reminds the father of his mortality.

Ideas, Themes and Issues

- **Father and son/parent and child**: The father and son have shared experiences which the son looks back on with fondness. It seems as though they find it difficult to talk to one another openly, and revert to familiar patterns and behaviour.
- **Mortality**: Removing the harmonium from the church reminds the father of his own mortality.

- **Regret**: The son regrets his reply to his father. The omission of his reply suggests guilt or shame.

Form, Structure and Language

- The **idioms** and **colloquial** phrases in the poem create a conversational tone. They make the way the harmonium is being discarded seem less brutal and may reflect a reluctance to address ageing and death directly.
- The **personification** of the harmonium links it with the father. This suggests they are both perceived as past their usefulness, but the son can't let either one go.
- The poet uses a reversed **simile**, with the comparison coming before the 'real' description. This suggests that the memory of the event is more significant than the event itself.

- In the final **stanza**, the use of the **present tense** creates a sense of immediacy and suggests that the son can't leave this memory in the past.
- **Internal rhyme** is used to create a sense of the heaviness of both the harmonium and of the subject of the father's mortality.
- **Sibilance** and **assonance** in the final line create a tone of self-reproach. This is emphasised by the fact that the son can't bring himself to directly quote his own words.

Quick Test

1. Why do you think the harmonium and church are named?
2. What is the effect of the consonance in the first stanza?
3. Find two examples of idioms that link to singing/music.
4. How does the metaphor in line 9 link to the end of the poem?

Sonnet 116

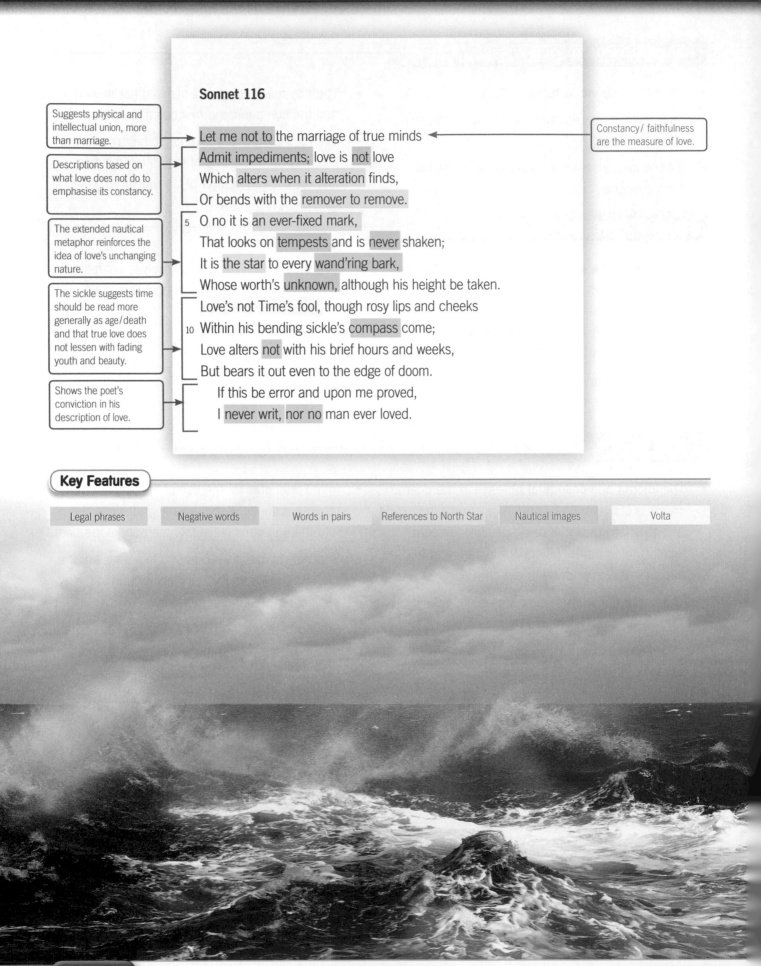

Sonnet 116

Suggests physical and intellectual union, more than marriage.

Descriptions based on what love does not do to emphasise its constancy.

The extended nautical metaphor reinforces the idea of love's unchanging nature.

The sickle suggests time should be read more generally as age/death and that true love does not lessen with fading youth and beauty.

Shows the poet's conviction in his description of love.

Constancy/ faithfulness are the measure of love.

Let me not to the marriage of true minds
Admit impediments; love is not love
Which alters when it alteration finds,
Or bends with the remover to remove.
5 O no it is an ever-fixed mark,
That looks on tempests and is never shaken;
It is the star to every wand'ring bark,
Whose worth's unknown, although his height be taken.
Love's not Time's fool, though rosy lips and cheeks
10 Within his bending sickle's compass come;
Love alters not with his brief hours and weeks,
But bears it out even to the edge of doom.
    If this be error and upon me proved,
    I never writ, nor no man ever loved.

Key Features

| Legal phrases | Negative words | Words in pairs | References to North Star | Nautical images | Volta |

Sonnet 116

About the Poem

- Written by **William Shakespeare** (1564–1616).
- Describes the poet's feelings about the nature of love.
- It is concerned with love as a concept and does not describe any place, person or event.

- The poem is structured into three **quatrains** and a couplet and has an ABAB CDCD EFEF GG rhyme scheme. **Sonnets** structured in this way are known as Shakespearean or English sonnets.

Ideas, Themes and Issues

- **Love**: The vision this poem presents of love as a powerful, ever-lasting force would have been seen as a **utopian** ideal at the time it was written, as marriages were often for social / financial reasons rather than for love.
- **Marriage**: In Elizabethan England, marriages were often arranged and had little to do with love. Men and women were not seen as equals and while love may have developed within a marriage, it was unusual to marry for love.

- **Time**: While time may change how we look, it is not an enemy to love. In fact, if love changes with the physical changes that time brings, it wasn't true love.
- **Loyalty and constancy:** Throughout the poem, there are references to the things that will not alter love, which shows its constant, unchanging nature.

Form, Structure and Language

- The **rhythm**, **rhyme** and **metre** are consistent throughout, reflecting the constancy of true love.
- The **quatrains** reveal different aspects of love. The first two describe its unchanging nature while the **volta**, or change in focus, after line 8 signals the change to a description of the long lasting nature of love. Most of the descriptions focus on what love does *not* do.
- In the first quatrain, words in pairs reflect the unity of love.

- Nautical **metaphors** link the idea of love to a voyage of discovery. The reference to the North Star suggests love's constancy.
- A nautical image in the third quatrain provides a connection to the previous ideas.
- Words from marriage vows and legal words remind us of the legal nature of marriage.

Quick Test

1. What is the effect of lines 5–8?
2. Which words and phrases bring marriage vows and legal practices to mind?
3. Summarise the meaning of the final couplet.
4. How does the voice in the poem describe the qualities of love, and what might this method suggest about the nature of love?

Sonnet 43

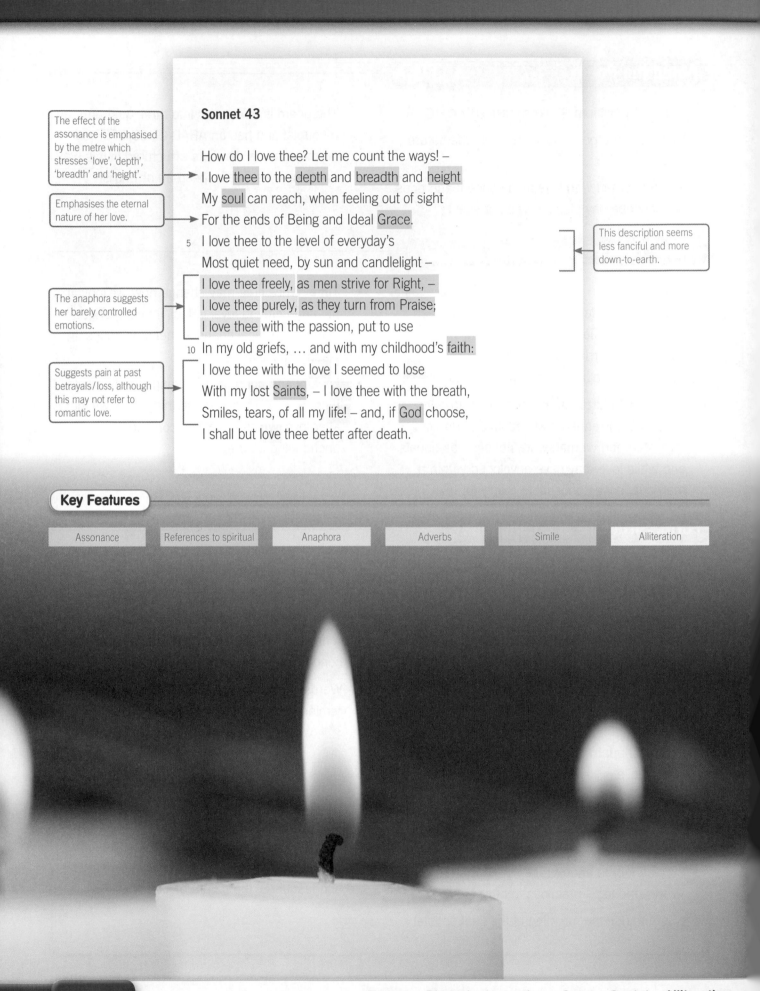

The effect of the assonance is emphasised by the metre which stresses 'love', 'depth', 'breadth' and 'height'.

Emphasises the eternal nature of her love.

This description seems less fanciful and more down-to-earth.

The anaphora suggests her barely controlled emotions.

Suggests pain at past betrayals / loss, although this may not refer to romantic love.

Sonnet 43

How do I love thee? Let me count the ways! –
I love thee to the depth and breadth and height
My soul can reach, when feeling out of sight
For the ends of Being and Ideal Grace.
5 I love thee to the level of everyday's
Most quiet need, by sun and candlelight –
I love thee freely, as men strive for Right, –
I love thee purely, as they turn from Praise;
I love thee with the passion, put to use
10 In my old griefs, … and with my childhood's faith:
I love thee with the love I seemed to lose
With my lost Saints, – I love thee with the breath,
Smiles, tears, of all my life! – and, if God choose,
I shall but love thee better after death.

Key Features

| Assonance | References to spiritual | Anaphora | Adverbs | Simile | Alliteration |

About the Poem

- Written by **Elizabeth Barrett Browning** (1806–1861).

- *Sonnet 43* is part of a collection of **sonnets**, *Sonnets from the Portuguese*, written for her husband-to-be. 'My little Portuguese' was a pet name he used for her.

- Although there are no references to the gender of either party, given the title of the collection we assume that this poem is about the poet's own feelings.

- Throughout the poem, she tries to explain the depth of her feelings and the different ways that her love presents itself.

Ideas, Themes and Issues

- **Love**: The focus on love is clear from the opening line. Throughout the poem, the voice explains the ways she experiences love and the strength of her feelings.

- **Mortality**: Death is not seen as a barrier to love. In fact, death will only strengthen her feelings.

Form, Structure and Language

- While the poem appears to open with a **rhetorical question**, the whole poem addresses and answers it, so it isn't rhetorical at all. The **exclamation mark** shows her enthusiasm.

- This poem is a **Petrarchan sonnet**. It is composed of an **octet** and a **sestet**.

- The **octet** relates love to political and religious ideals.

- The **sestet** compares her feelings now to her previous experiences, which were characterised by loss. These losses are highlighted through **alliteration**.

- **Assonance** in the second line mimics breathlessness. The stresses in this line highlight the **metaphor** which 'measures' her feelings.

- There are lots of words with religious or spiritual associations. This reflects the significance of this love to her.

- **Anaphora** is used to build **rhythm** and helps display the intensity of her feelings; no **synonyms** dilute the strength of the words.

- The simplicity of the final line contrasts with the rest of the poem and highlights the sincerity of the sentiment.

Quick Test

1. How would you describe the voice in the poem's previous experiences of love?

2. What is the effect of the line, 'I love thee to the depth and breadth and height / My soul can reach'?

3. What does the final line mean?

4. How does the poem's structure reflect the speaker's enthusiasm for the task at hand?

Assonance • Metaphor • Anaphora • Synonym

To His Coy Mistress

About the Poem

- Written by **Andrew Marvell** (1621–1678).

- The relationship is between a man and woman who are romantically involved but have not had sex.

- The poem is a **first person monologue** and the voice we hear is that of a man trying to persuade his mistress to sleep with him.

- He uses a different technique in each **stanza** to persuade her. In the first he uses flattery, in the second he uses pressure / threats, and in the final stanza he describes his preferred outcome.

Ideas, Themes and Issues

- *Carpe diem*: Latin for 'seize the day'. The man urges his mistress to act now while they are both young and beautiful as life is too short for a lengthy courtship.

- **Desire and passion**: His desire is clear in his attempts to persuade her to sleep with him. There is also a suggestion that she feels the same urge, but is resisting it.

- **Youth and beauty**: This seems to be one of the main causes for the man's pursuit of the lady.

- **Time and mortality**: His main argument centres around the pressure of time acting against them. Time is portrayed as the enemy of passion and desire.

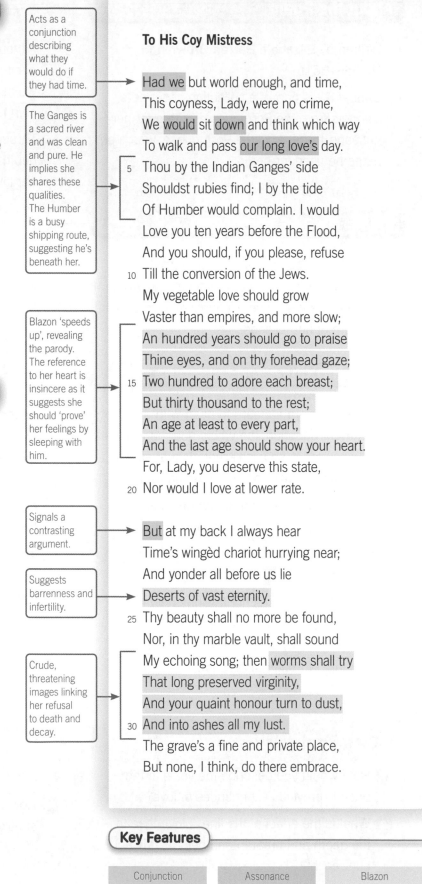

Acts as a conjunction describing what they would do if they had time.

The Ganges is a sacred river and was clean and pure. He implies she shares these qualities. The Humber is a busy shipping route, suggesting he's beneath her.

Blazon 'speeds up', revealing the parody. The reference to her heart is insincere as it suggests she should 'prove' her feelings by sleeping with him.

Signals a contrasting argument.

Suggests barrenness and infertility.

Crude, threatening images linking her refusal to death and decay.

To His Coy Mistress

Had we but world enough, and time,
This coyness, Lady, were no crime,
We would sit down and think which way
To walk and pass our long love's day.
5 Thou by the Indian Ganges' side
Shouldst rubies find; I by the tide
Of Humber would complain. I would
Love you ten years before the Flood,
And you should, if you please, refuse
10 Till the conversion of the Jews.
My vegetable love should grow
Vaster than empires, and more slow;
An hundred years should go to praise
Thine eyes, and on thy forehead gaze;
15 Two hundred to adore each breast;
But thirty thousand to the rest;
An age at least to every part,
And the last age should show your heart.
For, Lady, you deserve this state,
20 Nor would I love at lower rate.

But at my back I always hear
Time's wingèd chariot hurrying near;
And yonder all before us lie
Deserts of vast eternity.
25 Thy beauty shall no more be found,
Nor, in thy marble vault, shall sound
My echoing song; then worms shall try
That long preserved virginity,
And your quaint honour turn to dust,
30 And into ashes all my lust.
The grave's a fine and private place,
But none, I think, do there embrace.

Key Features

| Conjunction | Assonance | Blazon |

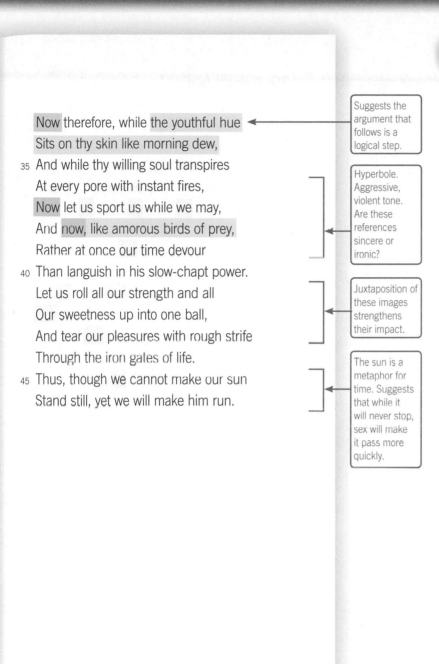

Now therefore, while the youthful hue
Sits on thy skin like morning dew,
35 And while thy willing soul transpires
At every pore with instant fires,
Now let us sport us while we may,
And now, like amorous birds of prey,
Rather at once our time devour
40 Than languish in his slow-chapt power.
Let us roll all our strength and all
Our sweetness up into one ball,
And tear our pleasures with rough strife
Through the iron gates of life.
45 Thus, though we cannot make our sun
Stand still, yet we will make him run.

Suggests the argument that follows is a logical step.

Hyperbole. Aggressive, violent tone. Are these references sincere or ironic?

Juxtaposition of these images strengthens their impact.

The sun is a metaphor for time. Suggests that while it will never stop, sex will make it pass more quickly.

Form, Structure and Language

- The title suggests the words have been overheard and are being reported to us by a third person. This distances the voice in the poem from the words and our reaction.

- **Conjunctions** at the start of each **stanza** reveal the structure of his argument.

- The idealistic, unhurried actions in the first stanza contrast with the urgency of the actions in the final stanza.

- He **parodies** and dismisses a poetic technique (the **blazon**), associated with love poetry, to question the idea of timeless love.

- **Assonance** in the first stanza slows the **metre** to match his descriptions.

- A range of **metaphors** linking sex and decay are used as threats.

- **Repetition** in the final stanza creates a sense of urgency for her to act.

- The **pronouns** in the final stanza suggest togetherness and unity.

- **Similes** are used in the final stanza, both to flatter her and to describe what he wants them to do, likening them to animals which act on instinct.

Quick Test

1. What is the significance of the biblical references in the first stanza?

2. What is suggested by the line 'Deserts of vast eternity'?

3. How are conjunctions used to structure his argument?

Imagery   Repetition   Pronouns

Blazon • Assonance • Metre • Pronoun • Simile

Key Words 25

The Farmer's Bride

- Written by **Charlotte Mew** (1869–1928).

- Describes the relationship between a farmer and his young wife. They have been married for three years, but their relationship is distant and is probably unconsummated.

- The girl responds to her husband and men in general with fear, and has withdrawn from the human world.

Ideas, Themes and Issues

- **Desire**: The farmer's desire for his wife is clear in the final stanza.

- **Marriage**: The marriage was not based on love or romance. The farmer seems to have chosen his wife on the basis of her age and looks. We assume that the wife had no say in the marriage.

- **Men and women**: There is a clear distinction between the sexes. While she is not close to the women, she sees them as less of a threat.

- **The natural world**: The poem is full of details from the natural world and the voice of the poem responds to the changes in the seasons. His descriptions of his wife compare her to a range of plants and animals. She finds solace and trust with animals.

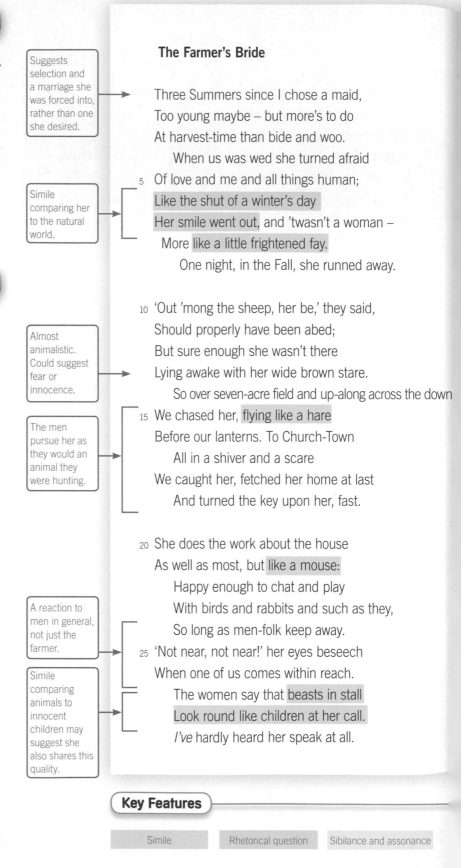

Suggests selection and a marriage she was forced into, rather than one she desired.

Simile comparing her to the natural world.

Almost animalistic. Could suggest fear or innocence.

The men pursue her as they would an animal they were hunting.

A reaction to men in general, not just the farmer.

Simile comparing animals to innocent children may suggest she also shares this quality.

The Farmer's Bride

Three Summers since I chose a maid,
Too young maybe – but more's to do
At harvest-time than bide and woo.
   When us was wed she turned afraid
5 Of love and me and all things human;
Like the shut of a winter's day
Her smile went out, and 'twasn't a woman –
   More like a little frightened fay.
     One night, in the Fall, she runned away.

10 'Out 'mong the sheep, her be,' they said,
Should properly have been abed;
But sure enough she wasn't there
Lying awake with her wide brown stare.
   So over seven-acre field and up-along across the down
15 We chased her, flying like a hare
Before our lanterns. To Church-Town
   All in a shiver and a scare
We caught her, fetched her home at last
     And turned the key upon her, fast.

20 She does the work about the house
As well as most, but like a mouse:
   Happy enough to chat and play
   With birds and rabbits and such as they,
   So long as men-folk keep away.
25 'Not near, not near!' her eyes beseech
When one of us comes within reach.
   The women say that beasts in stall
   Look round like children at her call.
   I've hardly heard her speak at all.

Key Features

| Simile | Rhetorical question | Sibilance and assonance |

30 Shy as a leveret, swift as he,
   Straight and slight as a young larch tree,
   Sweet as the first wild violets, she,
   To her wild self. But what to me?

   The short days shorten and the oaks are brown,
35   The blue smoke rises to the low grey sky,
   One leaf in the still air falls slowly down,
      A magpie's spotted feathers lie
   On the black earth spread white with rime,
   The berries redden up to Christmas-time.
40   What's Christmas-time without there be
   Some other in the house than we!

      She sleeps up in the attic there
      Alone, poor maid. 'Tis but a stair
   Betwixt us. Oh! my God! the down,
45   The soft young down of her, the brown,
   The brown of her – her eyes, her hair, her hair!

Condensed list of similes makes his admiration clear.

Slower pace suggests the farmer's ease with the natural world and contrasts with his feelings about his marriage.

Exclamation, repetition and internal rhyme suggest his torment/desire.

Form, Structure and Language

- The **first person monologue** presents the farmer's understanding of his relationship with his wife.

- The wife is described through a variety of **similes** comparing her to animals, plants and a fairy. This distances her from the human world.

- **Rhetorical questions** show his confusion. He seems lonely and the marriage has not given him the children or companionship he wanted.

- The farmer describes the changing seasons; he understands the natural world better than he understands his wife.

- **Sibilance** and **assonance** slow the pace as the seasons change to winter.

- **Enjambment** and an initial **caesura** highlight her isolation and suggest the farmer's sympathy.

- **Repetition** and **internal rhyme** in the final stanza suggest the farmer is tormented by his desire for his wife.

- Both the farmer and his bride understand the natural world but this only makes their difficulties more poignant.

Quick Test

1. Name three things that the wife is compared to through simile.

2. What phrases link the wife to prey being hunted?

3. What is ironic about the wife being described in animal imagery?

Caesura   Internal rhyme   Repetition

Sibilance • Assonance • Enjambment • Caesura

Sister Maude

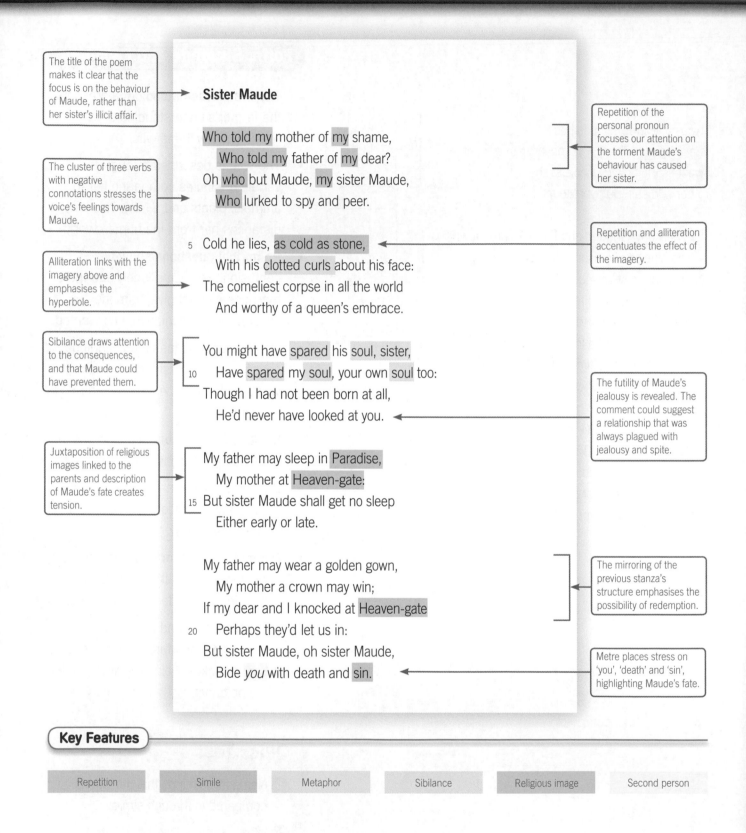

The title of the poem makes it clear that the focus is on the behaviour of Maude, rather than her sister's illicit affair.

The cluster of three verbs with negative connotations stresses the voice's feelings towards Maude.

Alliteration links with the imagery above and emphasises the hyperbole.

Sibilance draws attention to the consequences, and that Maude could have prevented them.

Juxtaposition of religious images linked to the parents and description of Maude's fate creates tension.

Sister Maude

Who told my mother of my shame,
   Who told my father of my dear?
Oh who but Maude, my sister Maude,
   Who lurked to spy and peer.

5 Cold he lies, as cold as stone,
   With his clotted curls about his face:
The comeliest corpse in all the world
   And worthy of a queen's embrace.

You might have spared his soul, sister,
10   Have spared my soul, your own soul too:
Though I had not been born at all,
   He'd never have looked at you.

My father may sleep in Paradise,
   My mother at Heaven-gate:
15 But sister Maude shall get no sleep
   Either early or late.

My father may wear a golden gown,
   My mother a crown may win;
If my dear and I knocked at Heaven-gate
20   Perhaps they'd let us in:
But sister Maude, oh sister Maude,
   Bide *you* with death and sin.

Repetition of the personal pronoun focuses our attention on the torment Maude's behaviour has caused her sister.

Repetition and alliteration accentuates the effect of the imagery.

The futility of Maude's jealousy is revealed. The comment could suggest a relationship that was always plagued with jealousy and spite.

The mirroring of the previous stanza's structure emphasises the possibility of redemption.

Metre places stress on 'you', 'death' and 'sin', highlighting Maude's fate.

Key Features

| Repetition | Simile | Metaphor | Sibilance | Religious image | Second person |

About the Poem

- Written by **Christina Georgina Rossetti** (1830–1894).

- The poem is based on a traditional **ballad**, *The Cruel Sister*, which tells the story of a jealous older sister who drowns her younger sister.

- Ballads were very popular in Victorian times. Alfred Lord Tennyson wrote a poem based on the same source.

- Deals with several relationships: romantic, sibling and parent/child.

- Maude is portrayed as a furtive/sly character who has caused the death of her sister's lover.

Ideas, Themes and Issues

- **Jealousy**: There are suggestions that Maude acted out of jealousy; perhaps she resented her sister's relationship. The voice of the poem suggests that her lover wouldn't have looked at Maude, even if she hadn't been there.

- **Siblings**: The main focus of the poem is the sibling relationship, which is plagued with jealousy and is neither supportive nor loving.

- **Sin**: Lots of souls have been damned because of the actions of the sisters. The souls of the younger sister and her lover have been lost because of their affair, while Maude's actions have damned her own soul too.

Form, Structure and Language

- **Repetition** in the first **stanza** emphasises the torment and exasperation of the voice of the poem.

- The **alliterative metaphor** in the second stanza emphasises the injury and links to the repetition and simile in the previous line.

- There are many religious images and references to religious ideas, reflecting the concerns of the time.

- **Sibilance** is used to show the younger sister's anger towards Maude.

- Maude is addressed in both the **second person** and in the **third person** which reveals the distance between the sisters.

- The final lines of the poem act as a **volta**. The **metre** places emphasis on the words that show Maude's fate.

Quick Test

1. What emotions are suggested in the first stanza and what techniques are used to suggest them?

2. What sins have been committed in this poem and who might be redeemed?

3. What emotion seems to have guided Maude's behaviour towards her sister?

4. What is the effect of the internal rhyme in lines 17–18?

Nettles

My son aged three fell in the nettle bed.
'Bed' seemed a curious name for those green spears,
That regiment of spite behind the shed:
It was no place for rest. With sobs and tears
5   The boy came seeking comfort and I saw
White blisters beaded on his tender skin.
We soothed him till his pain was not so raw.
At last he offered us a watery grin,
And then I took my hook and honed the blade
10 And went outside and slashed in fury with it
Till not a nettle in that fierce parade
Stood upright any more. Next task: I lit
A funeral pyre to burn the fallen dead.
But in two weeks the busy sun and rain
15 Had called up tall recruits behind the shed:
My son would often feel sharp wounds again.

Annotations:

Compare with line 5.

Internal rhyme and alliteration emphasise his preparation.

Onomatopoeia emphasises the action.

Melancholic tone created by the realisation of his inability to protect his son.

Suggests contradiction between the word's connotations and the pain the nettles within them cause.

Consonance and alliteration of soft sounds are emotive and suggest tenderness.

Alliteration links the words associated with violence and anger.

End-stopped line highlights the military sounding language and imagery.

Key Features

| Military words | Consonance | Emotive language | Onomatopoeia | Alliteration | Internal rhyme |

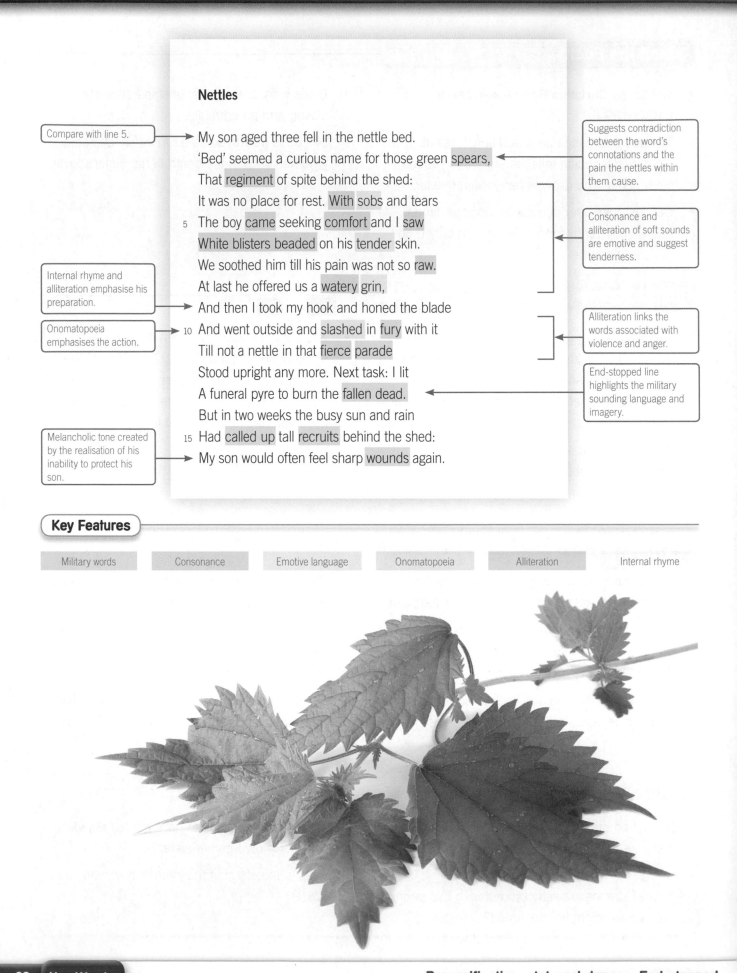

Personification • Internal rhyme • End-stopped

About the Poem

- Written by **Vernon Scannell** (1922–2007).
- Scannell fought in World War II and deserted twice.
- The poem recalls a childhood incident, where a father tended his young son after he fell into a nettle bed.

- The nettles are **personified** as soldiers and are described with words associated with the military.
- The father destroys the nettles but the futility of this action is clear as they soon grow back.

Ideas, Themes and Issues

- **Parenting**: A parent's instinct is to protect their child from pain, but this poem reveals the futility of that aim.
- **War**: The poem could be interpreted as a protest against wars that force young men to fight and to sacrifice themselves.

- **Violence, injury and pain**: The violent words describe the father's attack on the nettles. His reaction seems out of proportion with his son's injury – is he angry at his failure to protect his son, or is he taking out his feelings towards the military on the nettles?

Form, Structure and Language

- The poem has a regular but unobtrusive **rhyme** scheme, which could reflect the continual but unobtrusive presence of the parent.
- **Internal rhyme** highlights the father's anger towards the nettles / the military and the pain they cause.
- The first line is **end-stopped**, slowing the reader and emphasising the **repetition** in the next line. This highlights the importance of the incident and the image.
- **Consonance** and **alliteration** are used to reflect the emotions and feelings of the father as he tends to his son.

- **Emotive** language shows the tenderness of the father's feelings towards the son. This is contrasted with violent words which describe his attack on the nettles.
- Elements of the father's attack on the nettles are military-like in their organisation.
- The futility of trying to protect children from all of life's pain is clear in the last three lines of the poem. The final line suggests that life will always be a source of pain.

Quick Test

1. What does the image of the 'funeral pyre' suggest about the nettles?

2. Is this poem purely about a childhood incident?

3. What is the effect of the consonance and alliteration in the poem?

4. What is interesting about the words 'The boy' at the start of line 5?

Consonance • Alliteration • Emotive

Born Yesterday

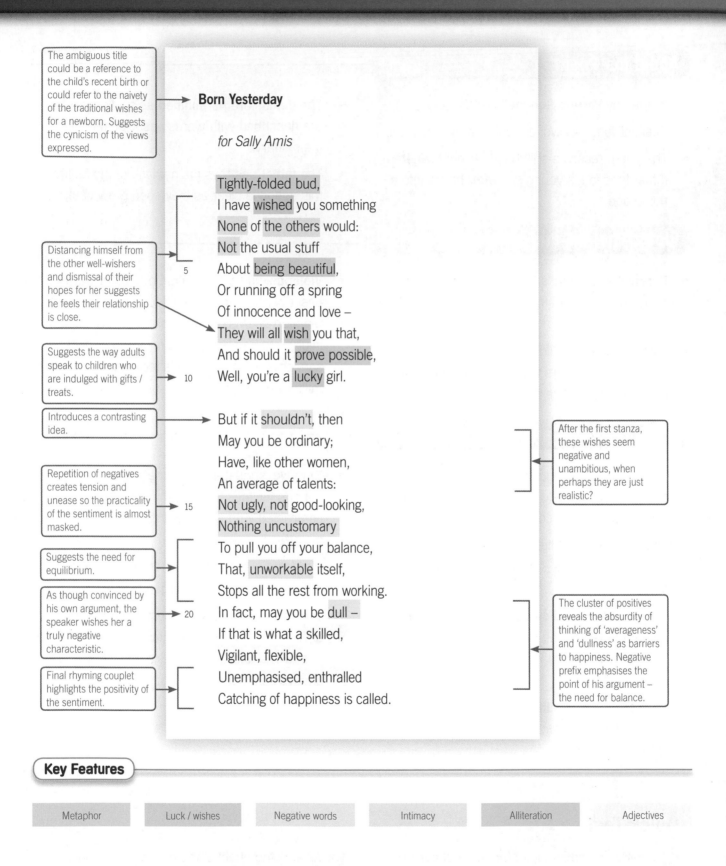

The ambiguous title could be a reference to the child's recent birth or could refer to the naivety of the traditional wishes for a newborn. Suggests the cynicism of the views expressed.

Born Yesterday

for Sally Amis

Tightly-folded bud,
I have wished you something
None of the others would:
Not the usual stuff
5   About being beautiful,
Or running off a spring
Of innocence and love –
They will all wish you that,
And should it prove possible,
10 Well, you're a lucky girl.

But if it shouldn't, then
May you be ordinary;
Have, like other women,
An average of talents:
15 Not ugly, not good-looking,
Nothing uncustomary
To pull you off your balance,
That, unworkable itself,
Stops all the rest from working.
20 In fact, may you be dull –
If that is what a skilled,
Vigilant, flexible,
Unemphasised, enthralled
Catching of happiness is called.

Distancing himself from the other well-wishers and dismissal of their hopes for her suggests he feels their relationship is close.

Suggests the way adults speak to children who are indulged with gifts / treats.

Introduces a contrasting idea.

Repetition of negatives creates tension and unease so the practicality of the sentiment is almost masked.

Suggests the need for equilibrium.

As though convinced by his own argument, the speaker wishes her a truly negative characteristic.

Final rhyming couplet highlights the positivity of the sentiment.

After the first stanza, these wishes seem negative and unambitious, when perhaps they are just realistic?

The cluster of positives reveals the absurdity of thinking of 'averageness' and 'dullness' as barriers to happiness. Negative prefix emphasises the point of his argument – the need for balance.

Key Features

Metaphor   Luck / wishes   Negative words   Intimacy   Alliteration   Adjectives

About the Poem

- Written by **Philip Larkin** (1922–1985).
- Larkin wrote this **free verse** poem for the newly born Sally Amis, daughter of his friend, Kingsley Amis.
- The poem expresses Larkin's wish for Sally's happiness, even if this means she lives a dull, ordinary life.
- His wishes appear to be at odds with the hopes and dreams that usually follow the birth of a child.

Ideas, Themes and Issues

- **Ordinariness**: While it seems that the talents and looks of ordinary women are criticised, they are in fact seen as a more likely way of achieving happiness than relying on beauty and love.
- **Luck and wishes**: The conventional wishes for a baby rely on luck and the poem suggests they are unlikely to come true. Even if they do, they are no guarantee of happiness.
- **Happiness**: Happiness is seen as fleeting and can be made more difficult to achieve if there is one 'special' thing about a person which unbalances them. While most people would want to be beautiful, talented and loved, none of these things in themselves create happiness.

Form, Structure and Language

- The structure of the poem creates **bathos** and suspense. The longer second **stanza** shows the importance of his wishes for the child.
- The opening **metaphor** is tender. It describes the folded limbs of a newborn baby and suggests the potential blossoming of the child.
- The distance he creates between himself and the other well wishers emphasises the unique bond he feels with the baby. Although he isn't the child's father, his feelings are almost paternal.
- **Alliteration** in the first stanza highlights his cynicism. The **plosive** sounds are harsh and mocking.
- Tension is created in the second stanza through the repetition of negative words and a **prefix** with negative associations.
- Lines 21–23 contain a list of positive **adjectives**, which make the meaning of his wishes clear.

Quick Test

1 How would you describe the poet's feelings for the child?

2 Explain the significance of the poem's title.

3 What is the effect of the half-rhyme in the poem?

4 What is significant about the final two lines of the poem?

About the Exam

What to Expect

The exam is divided into two sections, Section A and Section B. **Section A focuses on the poetry from the *Moon on the Tides* anthology** and Section B focuses on unseen poetry.

The poems in the *Moon on the Tides* anthology are divided into four clusters:

- **Character and Voice**
- **Place**
- **Conflict**
- **Relationships**

Each cluster contains 15 poems. Some of these poems are from the **Literary Heritage** and some are **contemporary**, including poems from different cultures.

There will be a **choice of two questions** for each cluster. You must choose **one** of the questions to answer. The question will **name one poem** and ask you to **compare** it to a poem of your choice. The poem you choose must be from the **same cluster**.

Some poems will only be named on one tier:

- *Hour, Harmonium, Sonnet 116* will only be named on the higher tier paper.
- *In Paris with You, Brothers, Sister Maude* will only be named on the foundation tier paper.

You will be given a copy of the anthology in the exam, but **it will not have any notes or annotations** on it.

What You Will Be Assessed On

In Section A you'll be assessed on how well you do the following:

AO1	**Respond to texts critically and imaginatively,** select and evaluate textual detail to illustrate and support interpretations.
AO2	Explain how **language, structure and form** contribute to writers' presentation of ideas, themes and settings.
AO3	Make **comparisons and explain links** between texts, evaluating writers' different ways of expressing meaning and achieving effects.

Your **spelling, punctuation and grammar** will also be awarded marks.

Remember that **you'll be awarded marks for the quality of your response** rather than for the number of points you make. It's far better to make **critical, insightful comments** than to merely point out the poet's techniques.

Allocating Your Time

You are advised to spend about 45 minutes on Section A. You could allocate your time as follows:

- **5–10 minutes** to **choose your question** and **make a plan**
- **30–35 minutes** to **write your answer**
- around **5 minutes** to **check your work** when you've finished.

About the Exam

Choosing Your Question

1. **Read both questions** for your cluster carefully.

2. **Highlight the key words** and think about how you would answer each question.

3. **Consider how much you know about the named poems and which poems** would offer the best comparison.

The table below suggests the main points of comparison between the poems in the cluster. It will help you identify poems to compare in the exam.

The crosses show the significant features of each poem so it is easy to see where the similarities and differences are.

		The Manhunt	Hour	In Paris with You	Quickdraw	Ghazal	Brothers	Praise Song for My Mother	Harmonium	Sonnet 116	Sonnet 43	To His Coy Mistress	The Farmer's Bride	Sister Maude	Nettles	Born Yesterday
Themes / Key ideas	Marriage	X								X			X			
	Violence / injury / pain	X			X										X	
	War	X													X	
	Love	X						X		X	X					
	Time / mortality		X						X	X	X	X				
	Passion / desire / sex		X	X	X	X							X	X		
	Regret						X		X							
	Trust / loyalty	X								X						
Form / structure	Sonnet		X							X	X					
	First person	X		X	X	X	X					X	X		X	
	Internal rhyme			X	X		X		X					X	X	
	Caesura		X	X	X							X	X			
Language	Imagery¹	X	X		X	X	X	X	X	X	X	X	X	X	X	X
	Sound effects²		X		X						X	X	X	X	X	X
	Repetition	X		X		X		X			X	X	X	X		
	Play-on-words / puns		X		X								X			
	Ambiguity		X	X		X										X
Relationships	Romantic / intimate	X	X	X	X	X				X	X	X	X			
	Parent							X	X						X	X³
	Sibling						X							X		
	Positive	X	X					X		X	X					X
	Negative			X	X		X		X			X	X	X	X	

Only the most obvious points of comparison are shown on this table. Use your knowledge of the poems to find unique features to create a personal response.

1 Simile/Metaphor/Personification/Onomatopoeia

2 Alliteration/Consonance/Sibilance/Homophones

3 Not a parent, but paternal feelings.

Planning Your Answer

How to Plan

Having a clear plan will help you to write a structured response and gives you something to refer back to if you get stuck while writing.

Your plan should be **brief and easy to read.**

In your plan, make notes about the following aspects of **both** poems:
- the **form** of the poem and the **narrative viewpoint**
- the **key ideas** or **themes**
- how the poem is **structured**
- the **language** used in the poem.

There's no need to go into a lot of detail or to write in full sentences. Use **key words and phrases** that will jog your memory when you look back at the plan. Make a note of the line references of quotations you could use to support your answer. If the quotations are very short, you could write down the whole thing.

Structure your plan in any way you want. You could use a **bullet-pointed list, table, mind map** or any other format that you're comfortable with.

As the time available in the exam is extremely limited, don't spend lots of time planning or writing an introduction or conclusion. An introductory sentence stating which poems you'll be comparing will be enough.

Here are some examples of page plans for a question comparing how a sense of desire is created in *Ghazal* and *To His Coy Mistress*.

Bullet-Pointed List

Creation of sense of desire: 'Ghazal' and 'To His Coy Mistress'

Form and address:
- *(G) Lover's exchanges in Arabic. Addresses the object of her affections, 'If I am... and you...'.*
- *(THCM) First person monologue. Directly addresses mistress: 'Had we'. Focuses our attention on his desire and methods.*

Language: Imagery:
- *(G) Metaphors: Rose and bird (1st sher) – natural, reciprocal, snake and charmer (4th sher) – wanting seduction.*
  Suggestion that desire is dangerous, 'moth to my flame'.
- *(THCM) Metaphors: 'your quaint honour turn to dust' (double meaning). Simile: 'like amorous birds of prey' – desire is aggressive and menacing.*

Structure:
- *(G) Mimics her desire for them – interwoven: 'you are the rhyme and I the refrain'.*
  Each sher can stand alone as an expression of her desire, but also contributes to the whole.
- *(THCM) Parody and rejection of blazon – desire too strong (lines 16–18).*
  Different technique used in each stanza – each represents an attempt at satisfying desire.

Tone:
- *(G) Conditional 'If' – wistful. Active verbs create erotic tone and reveal desire to be seduced – 'woo', 'subdue', 'bedew', 'renew', 'tattoo'.*
- *(THCM) Varies throughout – flattering (line 19), aggressive (line 27–28), urgent (line 39). All reflect his desire to seduce by any means necessary.*

Table

Creation of sense of desire	'Ghazal'	'To His Coy Mistress'
Form and address	Ghazal – 'lover's exchanges' in Arabic. Addresses the object of her affections, 'If I am… and you…'.	First person monologue directly addresses mistress: 'Had we'. Focuses attention on desire and methods.
Language: Imagery	Metaphors: Rose and bird (1st sher) – natural, reciprocal; snake and charmer (4th sher) – wanting seduction. Suggestion that desire is dangerous 'moth to my flame'.	Metaphors: 'your quaint honour turn to dust' (double meaning). Simile: 'like amorous birds of prey' – desire is aggressive and menacing.
Structure	Mimics her desire for them – interwoven: 'you are the rhyme and I the refrain' – like the lovers. Each sher has different image(s) but all contribute to the expression of her desire.	Parodies a blazon (traditional form of love poetry) and rejects it – desire too strong. (Lines 16–18) Different technique used in each stanza but all represent an attempt at satisfying his desire.
Tone	Conditional 'If' – wistful throughout. Active verbs create erotic tone and reveal desire to be seduced – 'woo', 'subdue', 'bedew', 'renew', 'tattoo'.	Varies throughout – flattering (line 19), aggressive (27–28), urgent (39). All reflect his desire to seduce.

Mind Map

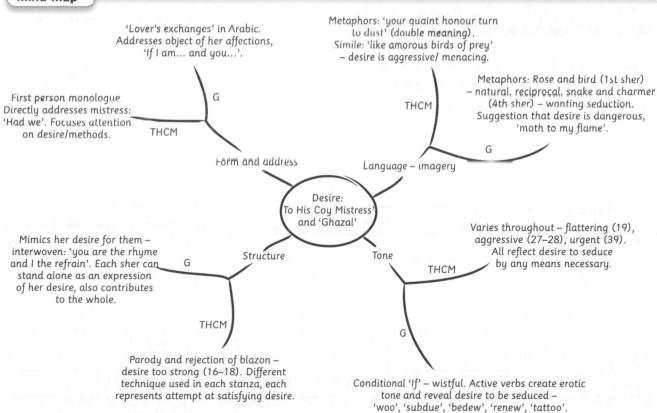

Writing a Comparative Essay

Finding Similarities and Differences

In your response to the question, you need to explain how the two poems are **similar** and how they are **different**, and **give examples** to back up your points.

As part of your revision, you could use a table like the one below to identify these similarities and differences. In each line make a brief note of the main points. Focus on identifying **interesting points of comparison** that you can explore in detail in the exam.

	Titles of poems go here	
	Similarities	Differences
Relationship		
Voice / viewpoint		
Themes		
Form		
Structure		
Language		
Tone		
My response		

Discourse markers

Discourse markers are the glue that holds your answer together. They show the examiner the relationship between your ideas and arguments. Some examples of discourse markers that you could use are given below.

To show comparison	Although	Conversely	Despite
	Equally	However	In contrast
	Similarly	Whereas	While

To add information	Furthermore	In addition	In fact
	Moreover	By the same token	In connection with this

To introduce an example	For example	For instance	Specifically
	This illustrates	This is demonstrated	In relation to this

Writing a Comparative Essay

Using Quotations

You'll need to select **details** from the poems to support the points you make. Choose your quotations carefully, keep them short and make sure they relate to the point you're making.

Always **aim to write as much as you can about each piece of quoted text**; there should be more of your words on the answer paper than the poet's.

For each quotation think about:

- the **techniques** the writer has used
- **what** this technique contributes to our understanding of the poem
- **why** the writer may have used this technique, i.e. the writer's purpose.

Shaping Your Paragraphs

The following example outlines a format that you could use to structure a comparative paragraph, looking at how a sense of desire is created in each poem. This approach will help to make your comparative points very clear.

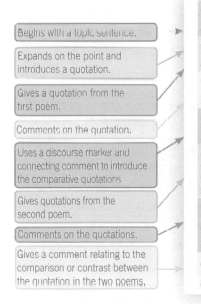

Begins with a topic sentence.

Expands on the point and introduces a quotation.

Gives a quotation from the first poem.

Comments on the quotation.

Uses a discourse marker and connecting comment to introduce the comparative quotations.

Gives quotations from the second poem.

Comments on the quotations.

Gives a comment relating to the comparison or contrast between the quotation in the two poems.

In both 'Ghazal' and 'To His Coy Mistress' the tone of the poem is important in creating a sense of the speaker's desire. In 'Ghazal', while there are variations in tone, there is repeated use of the conditional at the start of many of the shers, as in: 'If I am the grass and you the breeze'. This creates an overriding tone of wistfulness. The repetition emphasises the yearning the speaker feels and while it appears that the desire is fanciful or wishful, it suggests nothing unpleasant. In contrast, the tone in 'Coy Mistress' is rather more changeable. In the first stanza, there is flattery in his claim that 'Lady, you deserve this state', which changes to aggression when he declares that 'worms shall try / That long preserved virginity'. The final stanza sees another change as he is seized by a sense of urgency and presses her to act 'at once'. These continual changes in tone reflect his desire to seduce her by any means necessary. The continued, and at times, aggressive, attempt to persuade her to give in to him reveals the insistence of his desire. Although the speakers in both poems feel a strong almost overwhelming desire, the tone that they create in presenting this desire is strikingly different.

Tips for Writing a Comparative Essay

- Make sure you understand what you're comparing - note the key words in the question.
- Try to write a **balanced** response: don't favour one poem over the other.
- Structure your answer by taking one aspect (e.g. imagery) and exploring it in both poems.
- Start a new paragraph for each aspect you compare.
- Use **discourse markers** to signal the relationship between your ideas.

- If two aspects are significantly different, don't shy away. Highlight the fact and explain why / what difference this makes to the way you respond to the poem.
- Ensure you **maintain the comparison** throughout your answer.
- Use **quotations** to support each point you make about the poems.

Foundation Tier

Compare the way poets present relationships in 'Sister Maude' and **one** other poem from 'Relationships'.

Remember to compare:

- what the relationships are like
- how the poets write about them.

(36 marks)

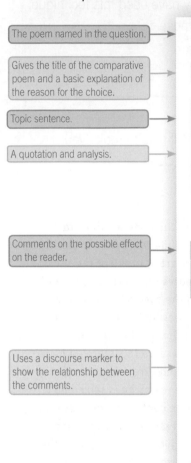

The poem named in the question.

Gives the title of the comparative poem and a basic explanation of the reason for the choice.

Topic sentence.

A quotation and analysis.

Comments on the possible effect on the reader.

Uses a discourse marker to show the relationship between the comments.

Makes a concluding comment which adds further comparison.

The poem 'Sister Maude' is about two sisters who have fallen out as the jealousy of the elder sister led to the death of the younger sister's lover. I am going to compare this poem to 'Brothers', which is also about a difficult sibling relationship.

The tone of both poems is clear straight away and helps us understand the relationship between the siblings. In 'Sister Maude', the repetition of the word, 'who' shows us the exasperation of the person speaking. The fact that she points out that Maude is her sister makes it sound really sad as ideally sisters wouldn't purposefully hurt each other. In 'Brothers', the speaker says he was 'saddled with' his brother for an afternoon. This suggests that he feels his brother is a burden and doesn't want to spend time with him. I think that if you were an adult reading this you might feel sad about this as you understand how important your family is, but most kids would prefer to spend time with their friends than their younger brothers or sisters.

In the poems, interesting verbs help us understand how the characters see their siblings. Maude 'lurked to spy and peer'; these verbs have negative associations and suggest she thinks Maude is sneaky. In a similar way, verbs are used effectively in 'Brothers'. The younger brother is described as he 'skipped' next to his brother, 'spouting' his opinions before he 'windmilled' home. These words are full of energy as the younger brother is excited at being with his older brother. The word 'spouting' is interesting as it is the only one that is negative, so in that way the poems are different as although he resents his brother being there, the description he gives of his brother's actions as he looks back on the incident is not putting the blame on his brother, whereas in 'Sister Maude' the voice we hear thinks the problems are definitely Maude's fault.

In both poems, sounds are used to reflect emotion. In 'Sister Maude' the speaker says 'You might have spared his soul sister, / Have spared my soul, your own soul too'. The hissing sibilance reflects her anger at Maude, who could have saved them all. In 'Brothers', rhyme in: 'His smile, like mine, said I was nine and he was ten' draws attention to how young he is. I think this means that we shouldn't judge him too harshly as he was only a child, doing what children do.

The final line often summarises the main idea of the poem. In 'Brothers', the speaker says; 'I ran on, unable to close the distance I'd set in motion'. The line has two meanings. At the time of the incident, it describes him not coming back to his brother as he follows his instincts to run off with Paul. As the poem was written by an adult looking back at his actions as a child, it can also mean the emotional distance that he thinks he caused by abandoning his brother. Similarly, in 'Sister Maude' the last line makes it very clear how the speaker feels. She says to her Maude, 'Bide <u>you</u> with <u>death</u> and <u>sin</u>'. These stressed words are very negative and show us she feels Maude has got the punishment she deserves.

Offers alternative interpretations.

Really good to comment on metre.

The sibling relationships in both poems have been damaged because of something that one of the siblings has done. The poets have used language and structure to show us how the speakers feel about their siblings. The main difference is that in 'Brothers' the voice we hear feels that they are responsible for the problems, whereas in 'Sister Maude' it is clear that Maude is entirely to blame.

A comment summarising the argument and relating to the question.

Again, relating back to the question but could be developed in more detail.

A final point highlighting a significant aspect of the comparison.

Examiner's Comments

This is a C-grade response. This student has used quotations and made some comments about how the writer's techniques might affect the reader. They have commented on the ideas and themes and identified some of the techniques that the poet has used to present the relationships, but their analysis could be more detailed. The response is well structured.

To achieve a C grade, you should:
- Compare the effect of language/structure/form and the way the choices the writer has made may affect the reader.
- Develop your analysis of quotations. It might help to choose shorter quotations in some instances, as this will ensure that the detail is analysed.
- Make sure that the similarities and differences in the poems are clear and that the comparison is sustained throughout the response.

Worked Sample Questions

Higher Tier

Some relationships give us a different perspective on the world. Compare how the characters in 'Hour' and **one** other poem from 'Relationships' see the world.

(36 marks)

Annotation	Text
Addresses the question.	
Refers to the first poem.	
Refers to the poem chosen for comparison.	
Outlines the main idea behind the response.	
Topic sentence sets out the paragraph's content.	

Relationships often create strong emotions, and can influence the way we perceive the world. The birth of a child and the experience of love have always been associated with a particular response to the world. In both Duffy's sonnet, 'Hour' , and Larkin's 'Born Yesterday' the response to the world is unexpected.

At first, both poems seem to conform to our expectations. The opening line of 'Born Yesterday' directly addresses the 'Tightly folded bud' of the newborn child. The tenderness of this metaphor suggests the folded pose of a newly born baby and reveals all the promise which the speaker feels this child holds. In 'Hour', the speaker describes her lover's 'hair / like treasure on the ground'. This simile suggests the preciousness of her lover; she is a valuable prize. As there is nothing unusual in these images and the sentiments they express, these images are comfortable for the reader.

Suggests the way a reader may respond.

Focuses on a 'small' detail. Titles are our first impression of a poem and their significance is often overlooked.

The titles of both poems are significant in revealing the characters' interpretation of the world around them. The ambiguous 'Born Yesterday', could be seen as a direct comment on the child's recent birth, or it could refer to the cynicism with which the wishes for the child's future are viewed. Similarly, 'Hour' can be read in two ways; as 'hour', the lovers' snatched moments of time are key, but, if the poem is read aloud, the word becomes the homophone 'our', signifying the lovers' focus on their relationship.

The way we interpret many events is influenced by our expectations and understanding of what is usual in the circumstances; both 'Hour' and 'Born Yesterday' reject the usual conventions. 'Flowers' and 'wine' are traditional, expected gifts from lovers. In 'Hour', the rejection of these tokens in favour of 'a grass ditch' is an anti-climax, the bathos highlighted by the full rhyme with the positive image of 'rich' love. The image is at odds with our expectations but this makes it all the more personal; it suggests the affair is furtive and the lovers have defined romance according to their experience. Just as our traditional expectations are rejected in 'Hour', Larkin rejects them for Sally in 'Born Yesterday'. The wishes for the child to be 'beautiful' and find 'love' are dismissed as 'the usual stuff', suggesting that he feels they are of little value. Instead, he wishes that she be 'average' and 'ordinary'. This jars with the reader as we expect any adult who loves a child to hope that that child grows up to be something special and extraordinary; the words associated with plainness seem at odds with the obvious care he has for the child. But Larkin warns that some things 'pull you off balance' and are in fact a barrier to happiness. Essentially, he wants the same things for her as 'the others' do – her happiness. His interpretation of the world is what makes his wish different.

Quotation integrated into the response.

Explores a small quotation in detail.

Sustained, insightful response.

Another similarity in the poems is in their structure in the final two lines. Typically, a sonnet like 'Hour' would end with a full rhyming couplet, but instead we find the near-rhyme of 'poor / straw'. The rhyming couplet at the end of a sonnet usually summarises the main theme or concern of the poem. In not conforming to the rhyme, the lovers are again showing that they define their relationship according to their own rules. In a similar manner, our expectations of the poem's structure are not met in 'Born Yesterday'. The full rhyme of 'enthralled / called' is one of few examples of full rhyme in the free verse poem. This draws our attention to the 'catching of happiness' that he wants for the child, and the way he sees her achieving it.

The way these relationships affect the characters' perceptions of the world is unusual. In these relationships, the characters' feelings cause them to depart from well-worn clichés; rejecting the idea that beauty and talent guarantee happiness and the grand gestures of 'conventional' romance. The unconventional views of these characters makes the poems intensely personal.

> Analysis of elements of a poem's structure should be included in any response.

> Comparative comment to link the poems.

> Comment relating back to the question.

> Comment summarising the comparison.

Examiner's Comments

This is an A*-grade response as it is analytical and exploratory. Well-chosen quotations have been analysed in detail to support the comments this student has made.

The structure of the response makes the comparison clear. Spelling, punctuation and grammar are accurate.

To achieve an A* you should:
- Include insightful comments and interpretations.
- Provide an *evaluative* comparison of the ideas, meanings, techniques, language, structure, form (where relevant) of the poem and the effects of these elements on readers.

Exam Practice Questions

Foundation Tier

1 Some relationships are difficult and unhappy. Compare the relationship in 'Sister Maude' and **one** other poem from 'Relationships'. Remember to compare:
- what makes the relationship difficult or unhappy
- how the poet shows this. *(36 marks)*

2 Some forms of poetry are traditionally about love. Compare the presentation of love in 'Sonnet 43' and **one** other poem from 'Relationships'. Remember to compare:
- the form of the poem
- how the poem's form helps us to understand the relationship. *(36 marks)*

3 Compare the presentation of family relationships in 'Brothers' and **one** other poem from 'Relationships'. Remember to compare:
- what type of family relationship is presented
- how the poem presents the relationship. *(36 marks)*

Higher Tier

1 Some of the poems use a particular relationship to explore a wider theme or concept. Compare the presentation of a concept in 'Sonnet 116' and **one** other poem from 'Relationships'. *(36 marks)*

2 Relationships often experience difficulties. Compare the way that characters respond to difficulties in their relationship in 'The Manhunt' and **one** other poem from 'Relationships'. *(36 marks)*

3 Sometimes a specific incident can influence the way we see a relationship. Compare how a specific incident affects the relationship in 'Harmonium' and **one** other poem from 'Relationships'. *(36 marks)*

Answers

These answers are only intended as a starting point and suggest 'obvious' comparisons. The tables show the main points of comparison; try to come up with some of your own ideas too, then pick four or five points of comparison and refer to the poems and find examples to analyse in detail.

Foundation Tier

1. You might compare *Sister Maude* with *The Farmer's Bride* or *Quickdraw*.

Sister Maude	Sibling relationship. Betrayal caused the death of the younger sister's lover. Maude is furtive and jealous. Repetition emphasises torment. Metaphor and alliteration highlight Maude's betrayal. Sibilance reveals anger. Metre emphasises Maude's fate.
The Farmer's Bride	Husband/wife relationship. Wife was 'chosen' and is young. She is hunted, caught and locked up. Similes distance her from the human world. Her fear is obvious. Enjambment and initial caesura highlight her isolation.
Quickdraw	A romantic relationship. Western conceit highlights the 'battle'. Passion and pain closely linked. Faltering rhythm mimics arguments. Internal rhyme and varied sentence lengths create tension. One person is affected more than the other.

2. You might compare *Sonnet 43* with *Hour* or *Ghazal*.

Sonnet 43	Sonnet – traditionally about love. Octet compares love to ideas important to the writer. Metre emphasises the depth of her feelings. Anaphora shows intensity of feelings. Final line has no internal punctuation so sounds sincere.
Hour	English or Shakespearean sonnet, differences to conventional rhyme and metre suggest problems. Caesura in final stanza reflects couple is concerned with the here and now. Juxtaposition creates bathos and feels anti-climactic.
Ghazal	Ghazal is Arabic for 'lover's exchanges'. Repetition creates wistful tone. Structure and content of the poem are interwoven. Rhyme highlights active, seductive words. 'Me' forms the refrain making it very personal and intense.

3. You might compare *Brothers* with *Praise Song for My Mother* or *Harmonium*.

Brothers	Sibling relationship (negative). Younger brother seen as a burden. Verbs emphasise different reactions. Ambiguity in final stanza. Caesura highlights distance. Short length of final stanza suggests regret.
Praise Song for My Mother	Mother-daughter relationship. Traditional African form, eulogising someone praiseworthy. Images suggest mother was child's whole world. The continuing influence of her mother is shown through '–ing'. Limitless love suggested through lack of punctuation.
Harmonium	Father-son relationship. Son can't part with harmonium or father. Harmonium symbolises their shared history. Inverted simile and present tense suggest importance of the memory. Sibilance, assonance and lack of inclusion of his words suggest guilt and self-reproach.

Higher Tier

1. You might compare *Sonnet 116* with *Praise Song for My Mother* or *To His Coy Mistress*.

Sonnet 116	Love. No references to any person, place, time, etc. Presents a utopian ideal, also suggested by 'perfect' sonnet form. Quatrains represent different aspects of love. Metaphors used to present 'qualities'.
Praise Song for My Mother	Motherhood. Reflects universal ideas alongside personal details. Link between mother and home. Metaphors show mother is child's whole world. Verb form suggests continuing influence of a mother's love. Shows the pull of a parent. Final line shows parent's sacrifice.
To His Coy Mistress	*Carpe diem* (seize the day). Opening of first stanza makes central idea clear. Blazon parodied. Time is personified as ever present enemy. Metaphors describe consequences of inaction. 'Languish' suggests weakness from inaction.

2. You might compare *The Manhunt* with *Quickdraw* or *In Paris with You*.

The Manhunt	Physical and emotional distance. The wife is searching for him. Rhyme scheme suggests fluctuations in couple's closeness. Repetition shows husband's reticence and wife's persistence. Verbs show developing tenderness and trust. Juxtaposition of sensuous and injury-related images creates tension. The wife's use of military phrases shows her connection to her husband. Unresolved ending.
Quickdraw	Western conceit highlights the 'battle'. Faltering rhythm mimics arguments. Internal rhyme and varied sentence lengths create tension. One person is hurt more than the other. Ambiguous ending – hurting or making up?
In Paris with You	Negative opening statement and repetition contribute to defensive tone. Altered syntax and made-up words suggest manipulation. Unwilling to commit. Conjunctions show changing emotions. Metonymy suggests a change in heart but reluctance/fear.

3. You might compare *Harmonium* with *Brothers* or *Nettles*.

Harmonium	Son 'rescues' the harmonium. Son can't part with it or his father. Harmonium is a symbol of shared history. Inverted simile shows the importance of the memory. Present tense suggests speaker is unable to leave the memory in the past. Sibilance, assonance and lack of inclusion of his words suggest guilt and self-reproach.
Brothers	Childhood incident retold through adult's perspective. Childish grammar and vocabulary. Younger brother a burden. Internal rhyme and metaphor remind us not to judge too harshly. Ambiguity in final stanza. Caesura highlights distance. Short final stanza suggests regret.
Nettles	Recalls an incident when young son is hurt. Consonance, alliteration and sibilance reflect emotions. Lots of emotive language. Futility of his actions is clear. Words to do with war suggest the incident has recalled other past painful experiences for the father.

Quick Test Answers

Example answers have been provided for the quick tests however they are intended as guidance only; wherever possible try to think of other comments and examples you could give in response to the questions.

Pages 4–5
1. 'porcelain' and 'parachute silk'. Both of these materials are delicate and suggest the frailty of the husband's body.
2. Through the repetition of 'after', the phrase 'only then', and in the repetition of the structure of the stanzas.
3. Through the verbs used to describe the way she explores her husband's body.

Pages 6–7
1. The extended metaphor linking the lovers to images of treasure and riches suggests that the lovers' time is precious and enriching.
2. 'a grass ditch' and 'cuckoo spit'.
3. King Midas and Rumplestiltskin. In both of these stories, the main character's greed for gold leads to their isolation and loneliness. This could suggest that the lovers' need for each other will isolate them from the rest of the world and that the relationship is somewhat doomed.
4. In a Shakespearean sonnet, we would expect the final couplet to have a full rhyme, adding to the summative feeling of the final lines. Duffy's use of half-rhyme sets the final couplet off balance and may suggest that the lovers' relationship isn't as idyllic as it first appears or that they continue to make the world fit their needs.

Pages 8–9
1. Substituting the word 'Paris' for 'love' is an example of metonymy and could be his way of showing his feelings without leaving himself open to be hurt. As Paris is considered a romantic city, his meaning is fairly clear.
2. The phrase suggests the hotel is disreputable and that the trip is little more than a 'dirty weekend'. It could also suggest how the voice in the poem views the relationship.
3. It gives the poem a down-to-earth feel. We can almost hear the words, as if they are being spoken directly to us.
4. The final line is significant as the metonymy of the final stanza and the previous one suggests that despite his best intentions, the voice in the poem has in fact fallen in love.

Pages 10–11
1. Phones and their voices.
2. 'the old Last Chance saloon'.
3. The lines are isolated on the page. The presentation makes them stand out and highlights their importance. If you read this as part of the conceit, the voice in the poem has been fatally wounded, and the other person has won the fight. In terms of the image of the heart as a symbol of romantic love, it suggests that the voice we hear has been left broken-hearted by the words of her lover.
4. The poem's mixture of enjambment and caesura, along with varied sentence lengths and unexpected internal rhyme creates an uneven rhythm which mirrors the unpredictable nature of the couple's argument and the erratic responses of the speaker. Caesura is also used in unexpected places to highlight key ideas: in the first line, initial caesura highlights the word 'alone', emphasising her isolation, and in the final stanza terminal caesura highlights 'I reel' adding impact to the statement and making the effect on the voice of the poem clear.

Pages 12–13
1. This line describes the structure of the poem and creates an image of interwoven lovers. The image suggests that the lover is as necessary to the speaker as the two elements are to the structure (and therefore, existence) of the poem. One cannot exist without the other.
2. This phrase suggests that the people in the poem have never been intimate.
3. That their relationship will be a turning point in their lives. The image also links back to the idea of poetry and creativity being fed by the relationship.
4. The rhyming words are all verbs, creating a sense of the lover as active and dynamic. Lots of these words suggest the voice in the poem wants to be seduced.

Pages 14–15
1. It sets the tone of the relationship and makes it clear that the older brother resents the presence of his younger brother.
2. **Any two of**: Younger brother: 'skipped', 'windmilled', 'spouting', 'spring'. Older brother: 'ambled', 'talking', 'sighed', 'stroll'.
3. The internal rhyme and the metaphor describing them chasing 'Olympic Gold' highlights their youth. These details may have been included so that we don't judge the older brother too harshly; they remind us that he was only a child too.

Pages 16–17
1. It suggests an outpouring of grief or that the voice in the poem is overwhelmed by her memories.
2. They show her qualities and attributes. They link the mother to her home and describe the things that she did.
3. It reflects that the mother's love is still felt. It could also symbolise the limitless love the daughter feels for her mother.
4. The imperative 'Go' in the final line suggests that the mother's love liberates her daughter and suggests a confidence in their love.

Pages 18–19
1. Naming them ties the poem to a specific place and event. This shows us that the events described are important and personal.
2. The consonance reflects the location of the poem, as churches are often quite places where people speak in hushed tones. The technique also suggests a reverence for both the place and the harmonium, probably due to the memories they both hold.
3. 'mine, for a song' and 'still struck a chord'.
4. The image foreshadows the end of the poem where, because of the nature of their relationship, the speaker is unable to reply to his father's comment in any way that does not now cause him regret.

Pages 20–21

1. These lines compare love to the North Star. Stars are used by sailors to work out their position so these images emphasise the constancy of love and suggest it is a guiding light to those who may be 'lost' without it.
2. 'admit impediments' and 'writ' suggest marriage vows and legality.
3. In the final couplet, the voice in the poem stakes his reputation on the truth of the ideas he has outlined. He also says that if this version of love is wrong, then nobody has actually ever been in love.
4. The voice in the poem describes love's qualities mainly by explaining what it does not do. It is only in the middle quatrain where this gives way to a description of what love does do. This makes the image of constancy in the quatrain stand out as the most important quality of love. The method used in the first and final quatrain might suggest that the exact nature of love is hard to pin down or exemplify without limiting it.

Pages 22–23

1. Her previous experiences were characterised by loss and sorrow.
2. This metaphor attempts to 'measure' a feeling against another immeasurable thing (her soul). In doing that, she shows that her love is, in fact, limitless and the image also suggests that her love for him is an essential part of her being.
3. The final line means that her love is eternal and ever-lasting.
4. The speaker's enthusiasm is highlighted in the first line by the caesura and the exclamation mark, which suggest that she cannot wait to answer the question and demonstrate her love. The poet also uses anaphora to emphasise the strength of her feelings. Enjambment also suggests intense feelings as lines flow from one to the next, without pause.

Pages 24–25

1. To show the length of time he would spend romancing her, if time was not a concern.
2. This image suggests a barren, infertile land, suggesting her fate if she refuses to sleep with him.
3. Although not a conjunction, in the first stanza, 'Had we', is used to describe what he would do, if time were no concern; it describes the expected rituals of romance. The second stanza begins with 'But' and signals that the ideas that follow will contrast with those outlined previously. In the final stanza, he opens with 'Now therefore', suggesting that the actions he describes are a logical consequence of all that he has previously explained and described. It appears that the only logical choice is to comply.

Pages 26–27

1. **Any three of**: a frightened fay, a hare, a mouse, a leveret, a young larch tree, wild violets, a winter's day.
2. In the second stanza, the farmer says 'We chased her' and 'We caught her'.
3. The farmer understands and admires nature, but his wife's response to her fear of men is to draw closer to animals and to distance herself from him.

Pages 28–29

1. In the first stanza, repetition of 'who' is used to highlight the torment of the person speaking. The repetition of 'Maude' and the addition of 'my sister', suggests a sense of betrayal.
2. The relationship between the younger sister and her lover is illicit but there is a suggestion that their sin might be forgiven. Maude's sin in causing the death of the lover is portrayed as unforgiveable.
3. Jealousy.
4. The internal rhyme links the images of the mother and father, uniting them as a couple. It could suggest that the sister hopes she and her lover may one day be united in a similar way.

Pages 30–31

1. The image of the 'funeral pyre' suggests a primitive but respectful treatment of the enemy. This links them again to soldiers, as the lives that soldiers lead are in many ways primitive/unsophisticated, but are characterised by a respect for 'the fallen dead', whether comrades or enemies.
2. The poem could also be seen as a protest against the futility of wars that are fed by constant streams of young recruits who become injured or die in battle.
3. These effects highlight the emotions in the poem. Consonance of hard letter sounds suggests anger, the alliteration mimics the child's reaction to the pain and tenderness with which the boy is treated.
4. The speaker uses the words 'my son' in the first and last lines of the poem. 'The boy' seems distant and the lack of the possessive pronoun 'my' suggests the poem is about more than the childhood incident.

Pages 32–33

1. There is a specialness to their relationship; it is distinct from that with the other visitors. The opening metaphor is very tender and shows the promise that he feels the baby has. His feelings are almost paternal.
2. It is ambiguous as it could refer to the recent birth of the baby, or to the naivety he feels the wishes bestowed on her show.
3. The half-rhyme reflects the fleeting nature of happiness and the difficulty in pinning it down.
4. The final two lines are a rhyming couplet – the only example of full rhyme in the poem – which emphasises the significance of the lines explaining his wish for her.

Glossary of Key Words

Adjectives – words that describe nouns.

Alliteration – repetition of a sound at the beginning of words.

Ambiguous – having more than one meaning (ambiguity).

Anaphora – repetition of a word or phrase at the beginning of successive lines.

Assonance – repetition of vowel sounds.

Ballad – a poem that tells a story. May have a repeated refrain, or chorus.

Bathos – anti-climax caused by a sudden change of focus from the extraordinary to the ordinary.

Blazon – a list of a loved-one's admired attributes. Usually describes the body.

Caesura – a pause in a line of poetry. Usually in the middle of a line but sometimes at the start (initial) or the end (terminal).

Colloquialism – informal language; the sort of language used in conversation. May include dialect words or phrases (colloquial).

Conceit – an extended metaphor that runs through a whole poem.

Conditional – use of the word 'if' to describe possible outcomes.

Conjunction – a word that joins phrases/ideas and shows the relationship between them.

Connotation – an idea or feeling associated with a word, phrase or object.

Consonance – repetition of similar consonant sounds.

Emotive – appealing to the emotions / evoking strong feelings.

Empathy – understanding someone else's feelings.

Emphatic – forcible, strong or clear.

End-stopped – the end of a sentence or clause coincides with the end of a line of poetry (the opposite of enjambment).

Enjambment – when a clause or sentence runs from one line of poetry to another, undisturbed by punctuation.

Eulogy – tribute to someone praiseworthy – usually someone who has recently died.

Extended metaphor – a metaphor that is developed through all or part of a poem.

First person – 'I', 'me' (singular), 'we', 'us' (plural).

Foreshadow – clues or hints that suggest what may happen later.

Free verse – poetry that does not conform to any particular form or structure.

Half rhyme – words where the rhyme is restricted to the consonants.

Homophones – words that sound the same but are spelt differently.

Idiom – a phrase whose meaning can't be understood by the words alone, e.g. 'to kick the bucket' means 'to die'.

Imagery – a collection of devices (including metaphor, simile, personification and onomatopoeia) which use language to create vivid visual descriptions.

Initial caesura – see **caesura**.

Internal rhyme – rhyme that occurs within a line of poetry.

Juxtaposition – the placing of (often contrasting) words or phrases next to each other.

Metaphor – a form of imagery where one thing is said to be another, suggesting similarities between the two.

Metonymy – substituting one word or phrase for another to represent the same thing.

Metre – the pattern of syllables and stresses that create a poem's rhythm, e.g. iambic pentameter.

Monologue – a poem where one person's voice is heard, often revealing aspects of their character and the situation.

Octet – a group of eight lines that may be linked by meaning and rhyme.

Onomatopoeia – words which, when spoken, echo their meaning, e.g. 'pop', 'splash'.

Parody – a mocking imitation.

Personification – a form of imagery that gives animals, ideas or inanimate objects human qualities (personified).

Plosive – consonants (t, k, p, d, g, b) formed by stopping then suddenly releasing air.

Prefix – an element at the start of a word that changes its meaning, e.g. un-, re-.

Present tense – used to describe actions in the present time.

Pronoun – a word that can be used instead of a noun e.g. 'I', 'he'/'she', 'they'.

Pun – a humorous play on words which depends on one word having multiple meanings or sounding the same as another.

Quatrain – a group of four lines linked by meaning and rhyme.

Refrain – a repeated phrase or word, similar to a chorus.

Rhetorical question – a question that answers itself / doesn't require an answer.

Rhyming couplet – two consecutive rhyming lines.

Second person – 'you'.

Sestet – a group of six lines that may be linked by meaning and rhyme.

Sibilance – repetition of 's' or 'z' sounds.

Simile – a direct comparison of one thing to another, using the words 'as', 'like' or 'than'.

Sonnet – a poem, often a love poem, consisting of fourteen lines.

Stanza – a group of lines in a poem that may have a shared meaning, metre or rhyme scheme.

Synonym – a word that means the same as another, e.g. closed / shut.

Syntax – the order of words in sentences.

Terminal caesura – see **caesura**.

Third person – a narrative viewpoint where the narrator is uninvolved and people are referred to as 'he', 'she' 'they', etc.

Verbs – words that describe an action or state.

Volta – a change in tone, focus or argument.